History in the Public Domain

RAZIUDDIN AQUIL

MANOHAR
2026

First published 2023

Reprinted 2026

ISBN 978-93-94262-14-0

Published by
Ajay Jain *for*
Manohar Publishers & Distributors
4753/23 Ansari Road, Daryaganj
New Delhi 110002

Typeset by
Ravi Shanker
Delhi 110095

Printed and bound in India

For

Professor Muzaffar Alam

CONTENTS

PREFACE

HISTORY IS A HOT topic in the politics of the public domain. In agenda-driven histories deployed in public debates, the question of truth is set aside in favour of requirements of the time. In such situations, history is not so much about the evidence regarding what exactly happened in the past, but a matter of opinion or perspective. This is the case both in vernacular histories circulated in the public domain and in the assumptions of professional academic history. Even though the primary functions of both are different, they converge in terms of offering differing vantage points in popular politics and struggles. Pressures from different kinds of ideological positions and politics of identities of various kinds together put serious constraints on the practice and writing of history.

Given the kind of myth and beliefs regularly thrown up as history and historians' quick dismissal of them as uninformed irrationalities, it is important to seriously analyse the objectives and parameters of professional academic history-writing and its separation from politically-motivated popular histories of the public domain. The controversial historical questions also need to be examined in a dispassionate and non-partisan manner. Popular histories serve as fodder in the political struggle for identities based on religion, caste, region, languages, etc. In these contestations, professional historical research is often set aside, and traditional notions and beliefs are privileged by the custodians of popular sentiments. Consequently, unverifiable social memories are preferred over verifiable historical evidence and facts; and history is misused or sacrificed in the quest for power.

On the other hand, despite contradictions between political ideologies and historical reality, as well as other challenges, academic research conducted and emerging from universities, research institutions, and journals, has been exploring new frontiers within the contours of history as a professional discipline. Relevant historical questions are analysed on the basis of evidence and its authenticity, validation, and corroboration. Even though social and political contexts of historians, their languages, theoretical models and assumptions determine historical interpretations and narratives, credible professional historians are expected to maintain objectivity and eschew biases and prejudices. Conducted in this manner, rigorous historical research as part of the discursive field of knowledge production is complete in itself and confirms the validity of its disciplinary practice.

This collection of short essays and extended discussions on current research aims to intervene in public debates on what exactly happened in history. Given the situation, attempts of this kind can possibly help in somewhat bridging the wide gap between serious academic research and misplaced assumptions of popular histories. Some dissemination of professional historical research in the public domain is not impossible. Much as historians are accused of merely speaking to themselves (and boring others), they need to be taken seriously when intervening in public debates using specialized historical methods and practices. Historical research conducted in universities can inform public debates in newspapers, television channels, social media and roadside *dhaba*s for that matter, to lift the discussion to an informed intellectual plank and to bring about historical literacy and civility in the public domain.

Some of the short essays and reviews included in this book have been previously published at different places, which are acknowledged at the end of each of the chapters. Some are also unpublished commentaries on books, or summaries of my lectures and talks, including a few recent Webinars. I had earlier posted these on my blog, *Itihasnama.*

I take the opportunity to gratefully acknowledge some of the finest editors who have published my articles and reviews in their publications: M.J. Akbar and Joyeeta Basu (*Sunday Guardian*), Seema Mustafa (*Citizen Online*), Rammanohar Reddy (*Economic and Political Weekly*), Bhaswati Chakravorty (*Telegraph*), Uttam Sengupta (*National Herald*), and Jayanthi Krishnamachary (*Frontline*).

I am also thankful to senior scholars in social sciences and humanities for inspiration with excellence in rigorous research and necessary intervention in public, when needed. Rajeev Bhargava, Neeladri Bhattacharya, Partha Chatterjee, Supriya Chaudhuri, Narayani Gupta, Mukul Kesavan, Harbans Mukhia, and Mahesh Rangarajan require special mention.

I would also like to thank David Curley, Jack Hawley and Werner Menski for their outstanding support and encouragement for long.

A number of colleagues and friends read everything I write: remembering to express my gratitude to Deeksha Bhardwaj, Prasun Chatterjee, Mimi Choudhury, Parul Pandya Dhar,

Amar Farooqui, Charu Gupta, Mazhar Hussain, Bharati Jagannathan, Anshu Malhotra, Rashmi Mishra, Shireen M. Mondal, Tilottama Mukherjee, Farhat Nasreen, Vipul Singh, and Chitralekha Zutshi.

Last but not the least, I am thinking how appropriate it is to offer this collection of essays as a small gift to Professor Muzaffar Alam, in whose association I learned so much as a research scholar in good old Jawaharlal Nehru University, New Delhi, even though the learned Professor is known for tact and reticence, whereas I like to tell it all, even when situation demands political correctness. There are moments in our history when scholars and intellectuals need to stick their neck out, calling a spade a spade. For, it is in the interest of our society and country that truth must prevail. This emphasis on returning to the facts of the matter is particularly urgent in the current post-truth era, which is creating so much ill-will and hatred around us. Thus, the essays also call for the much needed peace in society.

University of Delhi RAZIUDDIN AQUIL
June 2022

1

INVOKING VIRTUES OF TRUTH: HAQ ALI ALI ALI MAULA ALI ALI

NAHJUL BALAGHA, OR THE Peak of Eloquence, contains a large number of sermons, letters and sayings of Imam Ali ibn abi Talib, cousin and son-in-law of Prophet Muhammad and the fourth of the rightly-guided caliphs in mid-seventh century Arabia. The compilation offers fine nuggets of advice on a whole range of matters relating to just and proper conduct. Addressed also as Hazrat Ali and Maula Ali, he is deeply venerated in most forms and *firqa*s, sects, of Islam, particularly in Shia and Sufi traditions; the *qawwali* musical practices especially invoke his charisma for creating powerful emotions and ecstasy. Just close your eyes and listen to music maestro Nusrat Fateh Ali Khan's emotionally-charged rendition of 'Haq Ali Ali Ali Maula Ali Ali', for a blissful escape from the miseries of life – with a feeling of mercy and kindness for all the beautiful creations of God and for some relief to one's own heart.

Hazrat Ali's sermons recorded in *Nahjul Balagha* seem eternally relevant and one of them on the 'Tongue as the Medium of Habitual Hypocrisy' is particularly instructive:

> Remember that you are passing through the sad times, in which there are only a few people who speak the truth; when speeches seldom contain the truth, and when those who speak out truth are humiliated and degraded. People are now bent upon vices and sins.

> Their habitual hypocrisy and pretension make them indulge in fake amity and friendship among themselves. The youth are ill-natured and wicked, and the elders are vicious sinners. Learned among them are divisive pretenders. Preachers among them are flatterers. Their young do not respect their elders. Their rich do not help the poor and have-nots.

Such insights on moral lapses and violations in times of political crisis that Hazrat Ali had to endure and which ultimately consumed him, are a reminder of how blind following of religious and spiritual leaders of our own time such as *guru*s, *baba*s and other wily pedlars of faith cannot take a society very far; their approach is generally narrowly sectarian and conservative, with no scope for critical thinking or questioning. This is especially true when religious leadership is usurped by people of dubious credentials, who do not hesitate to abuse political power and exploit popular sentiments to reinforce their claims to authority.

In such a situation and always, it is better to be a liberal in a broad-based political and cultural context facilitated by responsible governance, providing space for tolerance of difference, guaranteeing freedom of speech and basic human rights – as we generally like to say, irrespective of caste or creed. On the other hand, the powers-that-be have the option of rising above religious or sectarian control to sustain a just kind of political order or get caught by the need for religious legitimacy for their illegitimate actions.

Hazrat Ali would have warned: Remember that every period has an end and every action a reaction; therefore, it is not only advisable but also imperative for you to separate truth from falsehood. He would emphasize: Remember in bad times society will be composed of ignoble and avaricious people, and generous and noble-minded people will be reduced to a small minority; people in such times will be like hungry wolves; the rulers will be like carnivorous beasts, ravenously devouring the middle classes and recklessly killing the poor; only lip service will remain because hypocrisy and hidden enmity will have a firm hold on the minds of people.

It is indeed time to rise above religious and sectarian differences and reflect on the kind of society we want to live in: violent and unjust or peaceful and with space for justice for all. There is a message for all here: rulers have to be responsible and committed to the idea of justice and good governance; interreligious wars need to be checked once and for all; and sectarian struggles, including Shia-Sunni kind, which weaken Muslim communities from within and fill them with ill-will, disrespect and dissensions, have to be abandoned in favour of peaceful coexistence. All these would require some sense of forgiveness, respect for and responsibilities towards all human beings as creatures of God.

In his book, *Animals in Islamic Tradition and Muslim Cultures*, Richard Foltz has quoted a statement attributed to Hazrat Ali:

> Happy is the one who leads the life of a dog! For the dog has ten characteristics which everyone should possess. First, the dog has no status among creatures; second, the dog is a pauper having no worldly goods; third, the entire earth is his resting place; fourth, the dog goes hungry most of the time; fifth, the dog will not leave his master's door even after receiving a hundred lashes; sixth, he protects his master and his friend, and when someone approaches he will attack

> the foe and let the friend pass; seventh, he guards his master by night, never sleeping; eighth, he performs most of his duties silently; ninth, he is content with whatever his master gives him; and, tenth, when he dies, he leaves no inheritance.

Dogs can, indeed, serve as a role model for people in our wretched times. As medieval saints and *bhakt*s would appeal: there is need to cleanse one's heart and discover a kind and merciful God within ourselves. And as Sufis devoted to Hazrat Ali would put it: service to humanity is the best kind of worship. Thus, all one needs to do is to show some small mercies for benefiting, at least, one's own heart.

REFERENCES

Nahjul Balagha or *The Peak of Eloquence: Sermons, Letters and Sayings of Imam Ali ibn abi Talib*, English tr. Askari Jafri, part I, Delhi: Alwaaz International, 2010.

Foltz, Richard C., *Animals in Islamic Tradition and Muslim Cultures*, Oxford: Oneworld Publications, 2007.

2

AUTHORITARIANISM IN THE GARB OF DEMOCRACY

EMINENT SOCIAL SCIENTIST Partha Chatterjee's recent lectures published in the book, *I am the People*, can help understand the havoc being created by authoritarian regimes everywhere. Backed by popular majority, the so-called strong and authoritarian leaders are determined to crush the marginalized and minority people in their own country. Dominate and shoot will be their *mantra* to deal with even peaceful protests against serious human rights violations by the agents of the state. If police cannot handle it, they will not hesitate to deploy the army to kill and suppress people into silence.

This is a kind of madness that defies all logic of the powers of the state, whatever their models. Both as sovereign power and government, the state must know its responsibilities: political stability, social peace and economic prosperity established in such a way that people are not discriminated against in the name of caste, creed or colour in a pluralistic society. Justice should be even in the sense that different sets of rules cannot be applied for different sets of people – law should be the same for everyone. If it is not ensured by those in power, they will lose the moral legitimacy to rule. This is especially true for regimes which organize genocide of its own people, and the police have the license to arbitrarily kill people from sections or communities identified as others in a cynical abuse of power.

Beyond a point threats of using the police and deployment of army do not work, especially when protests and resistance acquire the form of a mass movement. Courts of justice may become dysfunctional for some time, when judges and courts follow government's orders in a devious inversion of roles and practice. If international courts and human rights conventions are also completely ignored, then, at least, in informal juridical language, there is hope in a thing called natural justice. This will take care of everyone – the whole society. It might also lead to armed conflict and a cycle of violence, which will eventually require peaceful negotiations and reconciliation – bringing the powerful to their knees.

Following Partha Chatterjee, one might say that populist politics is throwing up strong and authoritarian leaders, who are expected to bring the economy back on track. Since such leaders lack proper education and expertise and do not even listen to any sound advice in the interest of the society – people, nation or state – they are unable to deliver. Instead, the problem is being deflected by holding racial or religious minorities responsible. This is creating a mess all around for serious repercussions to the democratic system itself.

But then dictators are not here for social service. They will kill people to remain in power, justifying their actions through external wars and internal othering – often conflating the two and presenting themselves as working in 'national interest'. Even serious diplomatic relations become a joke or dirty game for them and their large mass of followers, real or virtual, active on social media, Whatsapp and more recently TikTok. Unfortunately, it is the racial, ethnic and religious minorities and the poor across sections of society which bear the brunt. That is what we are seeing in the United States and in many other parts of the world today. They will go after having done a lot of damage to everything cherished. Darker days are ahead before sanity is restored and re-construction of social and political systems undertaken – a new order of things where justice and peace prevails, where innocent people are not killed in broad daylight, nor harassed on trumped up charges.

Unfortunately, the current round of mess is happening amidst a deadly Covid-19 attack, which is primarily consuming weaker sections of the population. Data is getting fudged, so it will be difficult to know for sure, but poor people, old, black, minorities, and unlisted immigrants who are not fully covered by health care facilities or protection are the primary victims. These are the people for the welfare of whom the neo-liberal state does not want to take responsibility. These are also the people who are most likely vulnerable to attacks of the kind that killed George Floyd. Therefore, the protest in the US was not an irrational reaction of a mob. The protesters were fighting against active discrimination and for equal rights. Reduced to bare minimum, racial, ethnic or religious minorities have a right to live.

In such contexts and always, the responsibilities of the state – social democratic welfare state or neo-liberal governmentality – is critical. This is irrespective of whether people are identified as citizens with sovereign rights in whose name governments are run or counted as a mass of surplus population whose interests and demands should be properly met. Instead of acting responsibly, leaders who have captured power on popular support are showing how pathetic they can get.

It is also too much to expect that people – popular majority suffering from 'sovereignty deficit' – who constitute the crowd that lynches human beings can make a wise choice about what kind of rulers they want. Enlightened leaders working for general public weal in an ethical state will remain a dream or ideal, as the mob, the crowd or the mass is unleashed and protected by those who control institutions of government.

For those at the other side of power relations, there is a long struggle ahead. Major transformation in political and social thinking for equal rights and thus recognized in institutions of law and governance will not be easily offered on a platter. The bottom-line is whether the state with all its power can ensure that its agents will not kill an innocent person. In other words, can one peacefully live without a threat to one's life? Unfortunately, neither history of political practices nor current circumstances are assuring us about even this bare minimum right to live. This will require some struggle.

As Partha Chatterjee would like to put it: the current crisis of leadership is the crisis of democracy itself – the picture is bleak, or dark, as the leader is working like a villain, instead of styling as a hero. According to Professor Chatterjee, combatting hateful environment in which right-wing thugs flourish will require a sustained intellectual argument for educating the rowdy masses of people and transforming them into more civil, law-abiding human beings, who can understand the virtues of peace and justice for all. It will be a long-term counter-hegemonic project. The road ahead is rough.

[Based on Partha Chatterjee, *I Am the People: Reflections on Popular Sovereignty Today*, Ranikhet: Permanent Black, 2020.]

3

POLITICS OF RELIGION AND THE WRITING OF HISTORY

HISTORY IS OFTEN used as a weapon in ideological struggles and identity-contestations. This is especially true in critical issues involving politics of religion. Within academia, religion and political culture profoundly impact the writing of history, leading to arguments, quarrels and formation of groups or schools of historiography. Thus, history of history-writing in India in the past couple of centuries has witnessed assumptions and formulations advanced from a number of standpoints. For instance, in colonial historiography – some strands of which have continued even till recent decades – colonialism was projected as something that was for the benefit of the colonized people; else, they would have remained savage barbarians with no or little sense of history. This false assertion was in conformity with the view that conquerors write history on the body of those they seek to dominate or decimate.

Countering the colonial position and showing that the conquered people eventually survive to tell their own story also, various strands of secular nationalist historiography have blamed the British colonial policies of nineteenth and first half of twentieth centuries for the mess the British left behind. Hindu-Muslim conflict, caste-system, economic degradation and a host of other issues are shown as constructed under the British rule. This set of scholarship also plays down the significance of religion in public life, even though it provides fodder for communal hatred and abuse. This is something which is aptly characterized by Professor Neeladri Bhattacharya – a much-respected Jawaharlal Nehru University (JNU) historian – as 'predicament of secular history'.

On the other hand, Hindu communal propaganda as history continues to take ugly turns. Even serious historians belonging to the rightist camp – few as they are – come up with outlandish propositions. The best example that comes to mind is projection of medieval India as a dark age in the right-wing historiography. It is asserted that medieval India was shrouded in darkness because there was no electricity in medieval India; this was because bigoted Muslim rulers followed Islam, which was against science!

By contrast, and yet supplementing communal Hindu narratives, is an equally bizarre Muslim separatist scholarship, which glorifies the Islamic past in the subcontinent. It traces separate Hindu-Muslim identities back to Arab conquest of Sindh early in the eighth century. Also, important historical figures such as Sant Kabir and Mughal emperor Akbar are treated as agents of Hinduism who sought to destroy the cause of Islam in the medieval period.

Thus, what we are generally confronted with is political propaganda peddled as history. Does it mean history-writing cannot be free from ideological control? Happily, more empirically sensitive and theoretically sophisticated researches in recent times have led to fresh thinking. This is sought to be blocked or resisted both by secularists and right-wing political propagandists, but scholarship has continued to grow in institutions both within India and the West – especially in the United States.

New research takes head-on communally sensitive issues such as temple desecration and the question of conversion of non-Muslims to Islam. The nature of state is being discussed with reference to rulers' concern for law and justice for all, peace and tranquillity, welfare mechanism as well as looking for India's own political theory based on secular principles, as in concerns of political theorists such as Rajeev Bhargava. New studies on Akbar and Aurangzeb analyse broad-based political framework, theory and policies, which are contrasted with narrow and exclusive political strategies abusing religion for the purpose. Historical examples and philosophical insights on governing principles are used to assert that when religious beliefs run into problems with secular principles of the state in multicultural or multi-religious contexts, the secular principles and progressive laws must be privileged, as shown recently by analytical philosopher, Akeel Bilgrami.

Further, questions are being raised about the need to reconsider the conventional periodization of Indian history in ancient (Sanskrit), medieval (Persian) and modern (English) times (with specific language of sources to be utilized). The older and simple formulations are being broken through richer source base, including judicious use of literature in the writing of history. For instance, Sufi *premakhyan* (poetry of love) of which Malik Muhammad Jaysi's *Padmavat* is one of the best examples, are being studied by historians and literary scholars in recent years. However, they are perhaps still not in a position to handle the muddle created in the name of artistic freedom or in the service of communal politics – as we have witnessed recently.

In popular devotional fields, the shared and disputed terrains of Sufi-Bhakti complex reveal faultlines fraught with possibilities for shrewd cultural negotiations and brutal political violence. Two examples which may be given here are of Yogi Gorakhnath's favourable attitude towards Sufis, who were perceived as belonging to the caste of Allah, and of Kabir's aggressive support to the newly found fad for vegetarianism in medieval India.

In conclusion, history is a hot topic in popular politics of the public domain. Medieval Indian history is an especially contested field. Pressures from different kinds of ideological positions and politics of identities of various kinds together put serious constraints on the practice and writing of history. As indicated above, despite the challenges, scholarship has continued to grow. Current historiographical thrusts illustrate how a whole range of themes and issues are dealt with by professional historians from a variety of perspectives with reference to sources and evidence. Critical issues relating to the complex interactions between religion and political culture are no longer being swept under the carpet.

[Based on the author's presentation in a Seminar in Gargi College, University of Delhi.]

4

LIBERALISM/DOGMATISM AND THE WRITING OF HISTORY

MUCH OF WHAT WAS said about medieval India in the late-nineteenth and early-twentieth centuries have turned out to be inaccurate, incomplete and even downright false and misleading propositions. We know British colonial administrators especially made a lot of untenable assertions about 'pre-colonial' India being barbarous, dark age, etc. Similarly, it is also possible that much of the contestations about medieval India in the late-twentieth and early-twenty-first centuries are bogus fabrications, relevant only to the politics of the present. Fifty years from now, with the context changing, historians may laugh at the irrationalities of our time.

Tolerant and free speech demands that contrary opinions are respected, for it is possible at the current stage of our knowledge that we may not know enough and, therefore, a contrary opinion may be more accurate. At least, let us consider the possibility that there may be a variety of perspectives and approaches through which we may have some approximation of truth relating to the past, rather than attempting to establish an absolute truth. On the other hand, adherents of different contemporary political ideologies and political propagandists with commitment to political interests of various ethnic groups might contest each other's understanding of the past and press for only one of them as epitomizing the truth. They might try to establish their understanding of the truth through a variety of strategies, ranging from outright academic dishonesty and academic stupidity to straightforward and obvious forms of academic suppression, as philosopher Akeel Bilgrami has recently delineated in his exposition on liberalism and the academia. What happens to the question of truth then? An attempt is being made here to grapple with the problem.

There are two kinds of limitations in the writing of history. One pertains to the interconnection between ideology and history. Religious and political ideologies deeply affect the writing of history. Various approaches are shaped by competing ideologies such as imperialism and nationalism in the colonial period and Marxism/secularism/communalism in more recent times. The respective 'schools' of historiography denigrate and thwart each other, through false assumptions, violent assertions and use of political power. The politically neutral kind of empirical approach with no commitment to any of the competing ideologies is also suppressed, though truth remains discounted in political neutrality or 'balanced' approach as well. The second problem relates to the abuse of history in the politics of identity. History is a major site, a battleground, or at least a weapon in the political struggles of identities based on religion, caste, region, and languages. In these contestations, a lot of crude political propaganda is peddled not only as historical memory, but also as authentic history.

Some of the themes in medieval Indian history, which are marred by struggles on ideological grounds and politics of identity, include extractive or inclusive nature of political and economic institutions, allegations of political violence and desecration of temples, Sufis' role in conversion and Islamicization, even as their presence was crucial in the making of a pluralistic society, forms of pre-colonial identities (syncertic or shared customary practices versus separate religious identities of Hindu, Muslim, Sikh, Christian, etc.), and the larger question of medieval legacies.

Thus, the study of history is not so much about what possibly might have happened in the past, but it is about struggles over competing claims on what the interested parties like to believe what must or should have happened; it is also a struggle between reason and faith, truth vs falsehood. Political pressures and political appointments will also continue.

After all, conquerors have always written histories on the body of those they have decimated. Compared to that, National Democratic Alliance (NDA)/United Progressive Alliance (UPA) determining and sponsoring divergent kinds of politically-motivated histories, not only at the level of school textbooks but also controlling platforms like the Indian Council of Historical Research (ICHR), is not such a big deal, even though the autonomy of the discipline of history is seriously compromised.

More crucial and disappointing is politics within academia, often of a very petty kind – struggles over topics of PhD thesis, research grants and fellowships, controlling academic journals and publishing houses, nepotism, corruption and group-politics in appointments, syllabus revision and reading list, arbitrary course allotment, unjust hurdles in promotions, etc. For those at the receiving end of the power relation, it can be simply a long period of frustration; once senior dons retire and go, the next generation takes over and plays the same dirty game.

[Earlier published in the *Sunday Guardian*: http://www.sunday-guardian.com/analysis/competing-pclaims-often-destroy-study-of-history.]

5

CHALLENGES TO THE WRITING OF HISTORY IN THE INDIAN VERNACULARS

CONTRARY TO THE British colonial assumptions, India has rich and varied literary and historical traditions. Historical works are to be found not only in the classical languages such as Sanskrit, Tamil and Persian, but also from the medieval period onward, in a variety of Indic vernaculars like Assamese, Bengali, Hindi, Kannada, Marathi and Urdu. The vast corpus of Indian historical literature might be divided on the basis of languages, or presented in a whole range of genres, they eventually acquired the status of an important set of sources. However, a large part of this literature, on the basis of its writing style alone, merits the label of being 'history' in its own right. *Itihas*, *purana*, *vanshavali*, *charit*, *buranji*, *bakhar*, and *tarikh* might be replete with myths and legends, might not pass the test of veracity of historical truth, or might not be strictly chronological, yet they present sufficiently large examples of historical consciousness and traditions in India. Just because they are different in style and language from modern Western historical method, they should not be dismissed as altogether ahistorical.

A major limitation of vernacular history is that it is used as a weapon in the political struggle for identity based on religion, caste, region and languages. In these contestations, professional historical research is often set aside, and traditional notions and beliefs are privileged by the custodians of popular sentiments. Consequently, unverifiable social memories are preferred over verifiable historical evidence and facts; and history is misused or sacrificed in the quest for power. On the other hand, despite contradictions between political ideologies and historical reality, as well as other challenges, academic research conducted and emerging from universities, research institutions and journals, has been exploring new frontiers within the contours of history as a professional discipline. Relevant historical questions are analysed on the basis of evidence and its authenticity, validation and corroboration. Even though social and political context of historians, their language, theoretical models and assumptions determine historical interpretations and narratives, credible professional historians are expected to maintain objectivity and eschew biases and prejudices.

Contemporary trends in historical research show that a lot of progress has been made in recent decades. Basing on a variety of sources in different languages and genres, interesting new research is being conducted on politics, religion, visual cultures, performance, gender, caste, identity, and regional aspirations. Much of the cutting-edge research is in English, with international discursive engagements. To an extent, in continuation with pre-colonial forms of history-writing, modern histories are also being produced in languages such as Bengali, Malayalam and Marathi, but their standard is generally not at par with English. The situation is far worse in north India where teaching and researches in Hindi is considered infra dig and for a language such as Urdu problems are compounded by political and communal overtones. The vernacular histories, therefore, tend to serve as fodder for popular debates and politics than contributing to the production of knowledge in any significant manner.

Since academic institutions cannot remain isolated from social and political activities in their surroundings, subjects of research and teaching are also influenced by their contemporary contexts. Still, there is a wide gulf between professional academic histories and popular vernacular histories, which has to be bridged. In the name of establishing Hindi as the pre-eminent national language, thousands of crores of public money is spent by the government annually, amidst allegations and protests of forcible imposition of Hindi over non-Hindi-speaking states as well as a silent decimation of various dialects in north India itself. However, in the academic sphere, privileging Hindi is a token gesture. Theses are actively discouraged from being written in Hindi, though signboards must be!

The paucity of serious academic research work in Hindi is an open secret. Textbooks are thirty-forty years old, original research work is not being written, journals are either absent or of inferior quality, and researchers are increasingly found lacking in linguistic skills. Lack of funds for research and publication is certainly a major challenge, but it has more to do with mindsets and intentions. An entrenched elite with pretensions to modernity has been running academic institutions since colonial times, which is not conducive for generation and wider dissemination of knowledge. The centres of learning are, often, regressive. Instead of encouraging liberal ideas, they are trapped in casteism, regionalism, religious communalism and gender biases, which are sometimes cloaked in the garb of influential political ideologies and fashionable theories. However, recent developments in various fields, including politics, sports and even academics, indicate that it is possible to overcome the obstacles. Some fascinating new histories are being created, reconstructed, or, if you like, fabricated.

[Earlier published in the *Sunday Guardian*: http://www.sunday-guardian.com/analysis/hindi-on-signboards-but-not-in-theses.]

6

CULTURAL PRODUCTIONS AND THE QUESTION OF IDENTITY

LANGUAGE AND RELIGION are two crucial matrices of culture, competing ideologies and politics of identities. They remain important analytical categories for understanding the significance of wide-ranging cultural practices and strategies, either as broad and inclusive notions of national identities, or exclusive and violent formations on separatist linguistic or religious lines. Religious practices and ideologies are expressed in cultural terms and are often articulated in vernacular literature and histories. Linguistic and religious identities then shape the politics of the time and place, which can be as true for Punjab as for Bengal or Maharashtra; surviving oppressive forms of politics from within becomes difficult and external critiques are often unacceptable. The issues raised above are central to the concerns of a fine collection of essays brought out by Anshu Malhotra and Farina Mir, *Punjab Reconsidered: History, Culture and Practice* (New Delhi: Oxford University Press, 2012).

Punjabi language epic-romances, or *qissa*s, circulated historically in both oral and textual forms, are a literary genre with representations of piety as its central motif. The *qissa*s are found at the interstices of different cultural and religious formations (Perso-Islamic and local Punjabi), and reveal a more inclusive practice of popular devotion, incorporating diversity of opinion, thought and belief within Hindu, Muslim, Sikh and Christian traditions, which either remains uncaptured in the analytical category of syncretism or gets neglected in communal histories. Privileging veneration of saints, nineteenth-century Punjabi *qissa*s were remarkably consistent in their representations of piety that accommodated all Punjabis, irrespective of differences of religion, class, or caste, displaying an all-encompassing regional cultural identity and not affected by the era's increasingly communal political environment. As Farina Mir has shown, it is, thus, at odds with Punjab's colonial history, the experience of Partition, as well as long-term Khalsa-centric attempts to cleanse the Sikh community of devotional practices deemed unacceptable to proper Sikh conduct in the nineteenth century, or earlier. From this perspective, the shared tradition of Punjabi *qissa*s is different from the more exclusive *Gurbilas* texts, celebrating the struggles and martyrdoms of Sikh *guru*s and also from the *Rahitnama*s on do's and don'ts on how to be a good Sikh – distinct from both Muslims and Hindus.

In contrast, a particularly interesting example of breaking free from narrow theological and cultural boundary-markers – by choice or circumstance – is Gulabdasi *panth*, viewed through a fascinating perspective of Piro, a Muslim prostitute of Lahore who came to live in the Gulabdasi establishment. The theology, cultural expression and social practice of the Gulabdasis indicated a wide-range of influences on them: monism of Vedanta through Sikh ascetic sects, Bhakti literary and devotional practices, and broad mystical and philosophical ideas of the Sufis. Treating syncretism as a useful analytic category in this case, which helps understand theological equivalences (between *dharma* and Shariat) and cultural conversations, or negotiations, between different religious traditions of Punjab (Hindus, Muslims, Sikhs), Anshu Malhotra has suggested that religious conflict, as highlighted by Piro, could not wipe out pluralistic attitudes altogether and could even highlight shared ethics and cultural values.

That such marginal individuals and groups as Piro and Gulabdasis survived to write their own stories, even histories, indicate that the dominant groups did not succeeded in completely decimating the body and history of the subordinated; that the region of Punjab does provide a space for shared or variegated cultural and religious traditions, even as religious identities of exclusive kinds assert, turn violent or abuse power during political crisis. Occasional slaughter of some millions of population notwithstanding, as in the wake of Partition or even a seemingly systematic cleansing of Muslims in the eighteenth century, extremist ideologies have not been able to sustain themselves beyond a point. The *sanjhi sanskriti* (composite culture) embedded in Punjabi language and literature and mediated by religious preceptors who do not subscribe to one dominant political ideology, has been an enduring feature of Punjabi history and culture.

We know through the history of the region of Punjab in the past one millennium, or more, that political upheaval through the preceding winter is necessarily followed by the celebration of life in spring. Violent separatist ideologies give way to shared cultural productions – literary and religious practices – in a more equitable political context, when Piro's voice can also be heard and when a broader ethnic identity, Punjabiyat (though no less a problematic category), lords over narrow religious considerations. Early in twentieth century, one of the most illustrious sons of the soil, Sir Muhammad Iqbal typically deployed the language of poetry for his political message, exhorting Punjabi landlords for breaking old and worn out customary barriers between tribes and communities for a larger unity, both religious and political:

butaane sha'ubo qabaa'il ko tod|
rasume kuhan ke salaasil ko tod||

Less iconoclastic and more inclusive is the veneration of Guru Nanak by Nazir Akbarabadi in the late-eighteenth and early-nineteenth century:

sab shish newa ardaas karo,
aur har dam bolo waahe guru.

More broadly, the question of identity – multiple, dual, or exclusive – can also be understood historically through religious, national and racial entry points as has been done by Benjamin Lieberman in an important work in global perspective, *Remaking Identities: God, Nation, and Race in World History* (Lanham: Rowman & Littlefield, 2013). Lieberman's book offers a rare combination of rigorous historical analysis and a fine narrative that will appeal to a wider readership, even though the theme involves dispassionately understanding terrible contestations over violent politics of identity for close to 1,500 years. As a fine historian of ethnic cleansing and genocide, the author has unpacked a variety of ways in which human identities have been created, transplanted and destroyed in the name of religion, nationalism or ethnicities. Identities could be large, exclusive, imagined, collective or dual and contradictory – all of them involved considerable political manipulation and mobilization, and though peaceful co-existence, appropriations and tolerance were the ideal, they often led to horrendous violence and destruction.

In this context, a thorough understanding of the making of the realm of Islam in seventh-century Arabia and the formation of an Islamic order in the Indian subcontinent since roughly the beginning of the thirteenth century is particularly significant. Moving away from the older Orientalist kind of politically-motivated approach of vilifying medieval Islamic traditions, Lieberman presents a more balanced, professional, academic and scholarly interpretation of a post-Orientalist historian. The discussion on Islam in India is especially important, as it highlights the complex ways in which medieval Islamic rulers and ideologues handled sensitive questions of crucial import, especially tricky issues of intermingling of religion and politics in diverse, multicultural contexts. It is also important for the appreciation of South Asian Islam as a major factor that policy analysts and others in the business of government would do well to understand. As a lesson from history, responsible governance based on a progressive law and an inclusive political theory can be the *mantra* for dealing with the crises involving failures of governments to resolve conflicts over religious and ethnic identities. A proper understanding of these themes and issues is critical in these times of xenophobia and resultant violence.

As the poet Iqbal painfully warned of a complete annihilation if voices were not raised against injustices and silencing under repressive political regimes:

na samjhoge tow mit jaoge ey hindusitan walo |
tumhari daastan tak na hogi daastanon mein ||

[Earlier published in *Citizen Online*: https://www.thecitizen.in/index.php/en/NewsDetail/index/9/1209/The-Question-of-Culture-And-Identity-Na-Samjhoge-to-Mit-Jaoge-ay-Hindustan-Waalon.]

7

RAMAYANA'S MULTIPLE TRADITIONS IN CROSS-CULTURAL CONTEXTS

MUCH AS POLITICS around Rama-bhakti has fallen to its nadir unfortunately, the scholarly endeavour to study the vast traditions of Rama stories is reaching the pinnacle of excellence. Some of the finest historians and scholars of literary traditions, visual cultures and performing arts have come together to showcase the results of their superlative scholarship dedicated to understanding the *Ramayana*'s myriad traditions. The distinguished editor and leading art historian, Professor Parul Pandya Dhar, has perceptively organized and contextualized the stupendous range of fascinating material on retelling the epic, encompassing several centuries and geographical boundaries across South and Southeast Asia – the longstanding connections between the two regions are determined by historical processes of epic proportions.

The early medieval connections have been studied by some fine scholars such as Hermann Kulke, Tansen Sen and Parul Pandya Dhar, among others. The value of the early modern connected history has been highlighted by J.F. Richards and in the voluminous writings of Sanjay Subrahmanyam in recent decades. The connections facilitated by large scale historical processes are to be seen not only in flourishing international trade and commerce, but also in circulations of texts, ideas, relics and gods across oceans and continents. Also remembering in this context, the fine work of Joseph Fletcher on integrated history, mapping vertical and horizontal developments for a global history of the early modern era. From within this broad perspective, the splendid product on offer – as many as nineteen chapters with a separate Introduction to savour – is a veritable treat for anyone with a heart for appreciating diverse tellings of the extraordinary credentials of Maryada Purushottam Sri Rama of Ayodhya. The equally fascinating character of Lanka's Ravana – the powerful anti-hero (and in some cases, a hero in his own right) – also comes alive in parts of the book spread over 370 pages. *Ravanayana*, as the editor put it, or *Ravanakhyan*, may be!

The editor and publisher deserve rich commendations for bringing together this marvellous collection of essays, placed in three distinct yet interrelated mediums of artistic expressions – spectacular visual representations, powerful literary compositions and tantalizing performance traditions. The book emerges out of an international conference on the multivalence of the epic, which was organized by Professor D.S. Achuta Rao Endowment in Bengaluru in 2017. The contributors include accomplished scholars of longstanding repute as well as erudite young researchers located across the world – including South and Southeast Asia, Europe and the United States. The meticulously produced volume as an example of awe-inspiring state of the art scholarship in a field of incredible dimensions, with over a hundred exquisite images, will also be a collector's delight.

The first section on visual cultures – sculptures, paintings, and inscriptions – comprises as many as eight magnificently illustrated articles, beginning with Parul Pandya Dhar's rigorous study of inscriptions and sculptures retelling the *Ramayana* in pre-Vijayanagara Karnataka. From around the fifth century onward, dynastic eulogies compare rulers with Rama as an ideal king, who is also represented in early inscriptions as a divine incarnation (*avatara*). These regional references to Rama and to Ravana – as a formidable adversary – reveal departures from the *Valmiki Ramayana* (dating broadly: seventh century BCE to third century CE). The next contribution by John Brockington emphasizes the significance of visual and inscriptional sources predating textual evidence of the Rama story in Southeast Asia. Yet visual imagery and inscriptions are also found side by side with texts since the late ninth century in Java, but much later in large parts of Southeast Asia, including Cambodia, Vietnam, Thailand and Myanmar, with possible connections from Bengal.

Valerie Gillet highlights the presence of Rama as an incarnation of Vishnu in the Pallava royal iconography, both in inscriptions and temple reliefs from Kanchipuram, in a milieu which sought to project the superiority of Shiva over Vishnu and Rama. The latter's presence in the royal discourse was subsequently asserted by the Cholas, who accorded significant space to the *Ramayana* in their visual repertoire. Further, Rachel Loizeau offers a fine reading of *Ramayana* in the rich Khmer sculptures with reference to the Yuddhakanda in Angkorian Cambodia, tenth-twelfth centuries, in a context in which there is a dearth of texts. The sculptures reveal complex adaptations, with new motifs inspired by local concerns, on the pediments and lintels of Hindu temples and Buddhist monuments – especially exalting chivalry and valour, besides depicting power to avert evil influences or bad luck.

Back in southern India, under the Cholas, *Ramayana* bronzes and sculptures, of Rama, Sita, Lakshmana and Hanuman, were deployed as important processional icons. A scientific-technical analysis of some of the key bronze icons by Sharada Srinivasan suggests that archaeo-metallurgical finger-printing of Chola period bronzes are distinct from the later Vijayanagara ones, even as the possibility of melting and recasting as well as fresh stylization indicates the need for understanding interesting complexities, both in terms of historical chronology and iconographic features. In continuation with the editor's approach of a back-and-forth movement to highlight inter-textual cross-referencing between South and Southeast Asian traditions, though within a broad chronology, the next chapter by Gauri Parimoo Krishnan draws our attention to the adaptation, localization and transformations in the character of Hanuman in Southeast Asia, in particular in Javanese, Khmer and Siamese portrayals. Styled variously as half-human–half-ape, puppet and dancer, with motifs drawn from visual and performance arts of varied cultural zones of Southeast Asia, Hanuman is presented as an intelligent being, artful lover, and playful magician in the service of Rama.

Further, in the centuries to come (sixteenth-seventeenth), the Nayaka rulers brought the idea of *rama-rajya* from their homeland in Vijayanagara to the Tamil-speaking region of southern India. The dual project of popularization and regionalization of the epic has been studied by R.K.K. Rajarajan with reference to the *Ramayana* paintings in the haloed precincts of the historic Maliruncolai Temple, connecting them with traditions relating to Tamil Alvar hymns of seventh-ninth centuries and with Kampan's twelfth-century *Iramavataram*. It thus becomes part of the larger subcontinental devotional tradition, a process intelligently mediated by the Nayakas. In line with understanding the multivalent contours of *Ramayana* traditions, transcending time and space, the last essay on visual cultures by Cheryl Thiruchelvam examines the continually evolving traditions of the *Ramayana* epic as expressed in different contemporary art forms in Malaysia. They range from traditional shadow-puppets to digitized characters and narrate episodes from the epic relevant to the specific socio-political and religious contexts of present-day Malaysia.

The second section of the volume on literary practices goes on to explore a huge archive of texts and their content, examining narrative accent and recitation, and showcasing associated imagery. Malini Saran highlights the significance of the discourse on governance and ethics as a leitmotif in the *Old Javanese Ramayana*, or the *Ramayana Kakawin* (ninth century), the oldest extant *Ramayana* text from Southeast Asia, which has followed a seventh-century Indian retelling of the *Ramayana*, poet Bhatti's *Ravanavadha* or *Bhattikavya*. As a Javanese text on ideal kingship, it goes on to have a life of its own greatly impacting later Islamic courts of Java and as a text meant for performance it also fused boundaries between textual and performative traditions. The next chapter by Chirapat Prapandvidya looks at the close links of *Thai Ramakien* (Sanskrit: *Ramakirti*) with south India, through connections with older traditions of *Ramayana* in Cambodia. In doing so, it digresses from the *Valmiki Ramayana*, which too was known in Thailand in the period between eleventh-thirteenth centuries. Surviving political violence, the current version of *Thai Ramakien* is attributed to the first ruler of the Chakri dynasty, who assumed the names of both Buddha and Rama – King Phra Buddha Yodfa Chulalok or King Rama I – and ruled from Bangkok during the period between 1782-1809. The Southeast Asian *Ramayana* tradition also includes the enigmatic character of the 'floating maiden', a *rakshasi* known as Benjakai or Srijeti, who is presented not only as counterfeiting a dead Sita to deceive Rama but is also portrayed in a romantic liaison with Hanuman. Mary Brockington deploys wide-ranging material to analyse the complex web of sharing and innovation of narrative elements and motifs from within Southeast Asian regions and across the ocean that produced the colourful character of the *rakshasi*, including a possible connection with the tenth-century Sanskrit drama, Rajashekhara's *Balaramayana.*

The next two chapters (12-13), in the section on literary cultures, look at *Ramayana* traditions in Malayalam. A.J. Thomas studies Tuncat Ezhuttaccan's *Adhyatma Ramayanam Kilippattu*, a sixteenth-seventeenth century Malayalam *bhakti* text aimed at offering spiritual solace to a people suffering from entrenched social exclusion and injustice, with no access to Sanskrit scriptures. Thomas offers a translation of excerpts from the text, in which Rama figures as the Supreme Deity, besides analysing its larger significance in Kerala society, which is reflected in its popularity down to modern times. Translation being an act of retelling, Sudha Gopalakrishnan presents a fine rendering in English of the critical Malayalam poetic composition, *Chintavishtayaya Sita* (Sita in Deep Contemplation) of Kumaran Asan (1873-1921), one of the Malayalam literary stalwarts. In exile with her two sons and

Valmiki, Kumaran Asan's Sita experiences her own agency, embracing truths about herself and Rama with grace and dignity, reconciling the agony of her exile with the warm comfort in the solitude of Valmiki's *ashrama* (hermitage), and considering the forest as a happier place. In Gopalakrishnan's moving translation, Sita's transformative self-realization meant a detached engagement, bordering on compassion, and withdrawal from the world:

> 'Do not worry, daughter!' With the sage's soothing words, gazing only at his feet,
>
> She walked on, her face bent downwards, and reached the royal assembly;
>
> Wordlessly, she went to him, saw her husband deeply drowned in remorse,
>
> Amidst the royal gathering, and in this manner, she relinquished the world.

The last chapter, in the section on literary cultures, by Thomas Hunter, highlights the deep connection between text and recitation with reference to the art of reading and interpreting the *Kakawin Ramayana* in Bali, to an audience gathered in club-like community groups, called Sekaha Mabasan. The stories recorded in textual sources are brought to life in masked dramas such as the *Wayang Wong*, devoted to the magically powerful characters of Rama and Sita. The narrations and performance in Mabasan clubs have led to a cultural reawakening and negotiation of Balinese identity in the context of tradition and modernity intersecting each other.

The representations of *Ramayana* stories in theatre, puppetry, and folk practices are dealt with in greater depth in the third section of the book on performance cultures. The veteran scholar of *Ramayana* studies, Paula Richman offers an interesting discussion of a couple of early modern and modern plays, which present Ravana in a sympathetic light, illuminating aspects seldom emphasized in Rama-centric narratives: a late-eighteenth-century Kathakali play in mixed Malayalam and Sanskrit, *Ravanodhbhavam* (*The Origins of Ravana*) by Kallaikulangara Raghava Pisharoty (1725-99) and a mid-twentieth-century Tamil mythological drama, *Ilankesawaram* (King of Lanka), performed to perfection for nearly 50 years by Lakshmi Narasimha 'Manohar' (1925-2006). Together, the plays offer an alternative political lens, commending Ravana's rule as centralized, but egalitarian, *ravana-rajya*, and departing from the conventional *rama-rajya*, without demeaning *varna* and *dharma* bound Rama.

Further departures are to be seen in Ghulam-Sarwar Yousof's discussion of the Malay Shadow play, *Wayang Kulit Kelantan*, said to be based on an oral version of the *Ramayana* from the north-eastern state of Kelantan on the Malay Peninsula, named *Hikayat Maharaja [Ra]Wana* (*Story of King Ravana*). These may be read in conjunction with the Malay-Indonesian *Hikayat Seri Rama* (*Story of Sri Rama*), among other Southeast Asian versions of the *Ramayana* stories – which in turn were informed by imports of several versions of episodes from the Rama saga, not only from Valmiki's *Ramayana*, but also Krittivasa's *Ramayana* (fifteenth century) and Tulsidas' *Ramacharitmanas* (sixteenth century). An interesting strand of the story analysed by Yousof narrates Ravana's misconduct in the Sky kingdom, which led to his banishment to earth and landing in Lanka, where he spent his time in penance. The Prophet Adam, who is sent down to Lanka by Allah, happens to meet Ravana. Adam intercedes on Ravana's behalf for his forgiveness and permission to become the ruler of three parts of the world, with the fourth reserved for Adam's own descendants. The story thus acquires a form relevant to popular Islam in the Malaysian archipelago.

The next two chapters in this section analyse versions of the epic in the Kannada vernacular. Krishna Murthy Hanuru examines how different folk performatives which popularised the *Ramayana* tradition, bringing it from palace to streets and bylanes, departed from the classic Sanskrit epic to suit the ideals of the folk world. This meant varying emphasis in the processes of idealization and demonization. Revealing complex relationships between classical traditions and the beliefs and aspirations of the common people, some folk performances tended to contradict widely held views on virtues associated with Rama and Sita, and yet others idealized the character of Hanuman. In the next chapter, Purushottama Bilimale, a distinguished scholar of Kannada folk and literary traditions, highlights the creative processes and improvizations by composers, musicians, actors and audience in the staging of the *Yakshagana* of coastal Karnataka. In Bilimale's words, together they continually recreate, redefine, communicate and appropriate episodes from the *Ramayana*.

The last chapter by Sirang Leng takes us across the ocean again for a discussion of the adoption of the *Ramayana* in *Reamker* performances, meant for both ritual invocations and entertainment in Cambodian Khmer society, where sculptures and inscriptions relating to the *Ramayana* are observed from as early as the sixth-seventh century. The history of *Reamker* performance dates back to the sixteenth century, with its popularity ranging from the high elite to ordinary folks – catering to the spiritual and social needs of the people, besides their entertainment quotients. The chapters on wide reception of performance cultures also reminded this writer of the excellent work of Philip Lutgendorf in the field and his translation and edition of Tulsidas' *Ramcharitmanas,* published as part of the very impressive Murthy Classical Library of India series. The recent work of Molly Kaushal, documenting local and tribal Ramalilas may also be mentioned here.

The Indian Sufi appreciation of versions of narratives around the ethical figure of Sri Rama of Ayodhya, from the fifteenth-sixteenth century, also add interesting dimensions to the common pool of literary and devotional resources around the cult of Rama. The devotional compositions of Sufi-Sant Kabir and of Malik Muhammad Jaysi of *Padmavat* fame as examples of Sufi adaptations of Sita-Rama narratives come to mind immediately. Awadhi Ramkatha in *Padmavat* predates its recording in the *Ramcharitmanas* of Tulsidas. And, for all we know, *Ramcharitmanas* is a Mughal text – and in Hindi, not Sanskrit. Interestingly, the classical period of Hindi literature coincides with the Mughal period, as shown in the fine work on the subject by Allison Busch. Mention may also be made here of the Persian translation of the *Ramayana* under Mughal emperor Akbar. Urdu translations have also followed in subsequent centuries. Hindu-Muslim binary around Rama-bhakti traditions is a political aberration, unfortunately. One is reminded here also of propositions pitting medieval *bhakti* traditions, including widespread devotion for the cult of Rama, in opposition to powerful Islamic presence as a somewhat flawed or misconstrued assumptions – Hindu resistance to Islamic rule in medieval India. This is negated by the fact that the retellings of the *Ramayana* in all their diversity have such a long history pre-dating the rise of Islam.

In conclusion, plurality and inclusiveness mark the enduring feature of the history of diverse *Ramayana* traditions traversing over two millennia and across wide geographical locations. The remarkable contributions to this significant volume have brought together many of the multifaceted features of the epic in south India and Southeast Asia. A sequel volume focusing on northern parts of the subcontinent, including Bangladesh, Nepal, Pakistan and Afghanistan will bring forth several other dimensions of the Rama stories. As Professor Dhar writes in her Introduction: Categories of intrinsic and extrinsic, change and continuity, classical and vernacular, and parts and whole offer useful perspectives to unravel the epic's multivalence. As it flows and adapts in varied contexts, its unique identity as a *mahakavya* (great poem) sustains even as it merges in a stream of continuous change. This assimilative power, with its diverse and plural renderings, is also its soul and strength. This reminds us of the heated debate on the value of the outstanding work of scholars such as A.K. Ramanujan and Paula Richman on many traditions of *Ramayana.*

As the annual Dussehra celebrations and current research illustrate, imaginative and powerful new tellings continue to be created, and the ways of perceiving them are many as well. Thus, to privilege any monolithic or exclusive reading of the vast traditions of the *Ramayana* is antithetical to its very essence. And as I like to put it: Let a thousand and one *Ramayana*s flourish!

[Comments on Parul Pandya Dhar, ed., *The Multivalence of an Epic: Retelling the Ramayana in South India and Southeast Asia*, Manipal: Manipal Universal Press, 2021. Presented in the 'Webinar on The Multivalence of the Ramayana: Texts and Recitations', organized by the International Research Division, India International Centre, New Delhi, 11 December 2021. An earlier version has been published in the *Frontline*, 3 December 2021.]

8

SANSKRIT HISTORICAL TRADITIONS: *RAJATARANGINI* OF KALHANA

THE PARTISAN HISTORIANS and political propagandists are involved in a circuitous debate on the historicity and dating of Sanskrit epics, *Ramayana* and *Mahabharata*. These classical texts are read like scriptures by sections of the believing masses and, though full of myths and legends, are celebrated as presenting an accurate account of India's distant past. The intertwined aspects of religion and history are part of popular-devotional memory for close to two millennia. Historians subscribing to modern, scientific and rational historical methods should recognize this as a fait accompli. A more serious appreciation of India's early history demands that attempts are made instead to read Kalhana's *Rajatarangini*, which offers a most fascinating example of history-writing in Sanskrit in the form of poetry (*kavya*), written in Kashmir in the middle of the twelfth century.

Indeed, if historians are seriously interested in exploring the notions of truth, chronologically arranged fine narrative of verifiable events of historical importance, surprisingly objective and unbiased accounts of matters involving even religious attitudes, and deploying a whole range of source-material as evidence, they can learn from the *Rajatarangini* of

Kalhana, at least in terms of understanding the method and practice of a historian of early medieval India, sounding completely modern, except that he wrote in Sanskrit and in the form of poetry. Unfortunately, Kalhana's text is not taken seriously by interested parties because of its non-religious and non-sectarian approach and it remains largely unpoliticized despite a few motivated translations, primarily in English. The author belonged to a Brahmin family of considerable political clout and is yet free from any prejudices against say Buddhists and Jains who were otherwise at the receiving end of Brahmanical reassertion in the period. In fact, Kalhana seamlessly transcends between early Hindu-mythic times and legends and a more credible specificity of Buddhist narratives in the latter part of his work.

It is important to recognize that Kalhana's history was not just a one-off example of a historical text oddly emerging from nowhere. The genre of historical tradition, styled as *Rajatarangini*, witnessed a number of scholars displaying their excellent expertise and it continued even under Muslim rulers all the way to the sixteenth century; the subsequent period also witnessed Persian and Urdu histories being modelled on the older Sanskrit form. Kalhana has written that he was wholly dissatisfied with the well-known works of history which were in circulation in his time – full of defects, ranging from limited source-base and missing chapters to factual inaccuracies and biased interpretations.

On his part, Kalhana was able to unearth neglected or even almost-lost sources relating to older kings, accessed all possible government documents, deployed tantalizing art-historical methods to study existing visual materials, and produce a brand new narrative of political and cultural significance with some candid observations on artistic language of poetry as the vehicle of sound political and cultural history. In his first chapter (*taranga*) Kalhana not only forgrounded his recovery of the lost rule of some 52 kings of Kashmir, which could help re-jig the chronology of India's ancient past, but also criticized the then prevalent assumption on the correct date of the battle of *Mahabharata*.

Kalhana insisted that only an accomplished poet can produce a fine narrative of a historical past in the language intelligible in the present; *kavya-amrit* or *rasa* being superior to the usual *amrit* and assured the readers that they will relish the *shaant-rasa* running through his text and sounding like music to the discerning ears. He also writes that catering to the taste of general readers interesting anecdotes have also been narrated at appropriate places, though he has cut-down the details for want of space. He pleads that his new interpretation or sort of 'revisionist' work on the history of Kashmir and by implication of the whole of India should not be dismissed as unimportant before reading or listening to it.

Of many things that Kalhana has observed regarding matters of current political interests, two may be mentioned here. First, he says, from time to time the country witnesses the rise of such blessed-souls as kings that their very presence leads to the removal of social-conflicts. The rulers who torture the subject, just vanish from the earth. By contrast, those who restore peace and prosperity in a backward country are able to perpetuate their rule and provide a stable government over a long period of time. He adds that people should learn about the distinctive character of kings of yore and back future rulers of the country accordingly. Second, and this seems extremely relevant at present, Kalhana has remarked that the people of Kashmir fear God, not any enemy, and added that they can be won over on the moral strength of good governance, and not through violent use of arms: *vijiyate punyabalaibaralaiyartu na shastrinaam* (*Rajatarangini*).

9

KHWAJA GHARIB NAWAZ MU'IN-UD-DIN CHISHTI: FOUNDER OF CHISHTI SUFISM IN INDIA

THE *DARGAH* OF patron saint of Hindustan, Khwaja Gharib Nawaz Mu'in-ud-Din Chishti at Ajmer in Rajasthan attracts a large number of disciples round the year. The annual *urs* (death anniversary) of the saint, especially witnesses lakhs of pilgrims, rich and poor alike, descending from all over and seeking blessings and benediction for a variety of purpose. Ritual Sufic *chadars* are also presented by leaders across the political spectrum in India as well as from abroad. The highlight of *urs* celebration in the year 2015 was the *chadar* offered by the then US President, Barack Obama, with prayers for peace and tolerance in a world marred by political violence in the name of religion. It is interesting to note that even Donald Trump sent *chadar* to the Chishti shrine subsequently.

The widespread veneration of Sufi figures like the Khwaja of Ajmer stems from the fact that they rose above traditional religious rituals and discriminations to speak in the language of love and tolerance for the whole of mankind. As the Sufis would say, everything is from God, whom they considered a friend, and since everything is God's creation, there is an aspect of God in everything – a position articulated in the doctrine of *wahdat-ul-wujud* (unity of existence). Viewed from this perspective, a little bit of love and respect for all of God's creations can take care of much of the difficulties in the world around us.

In his lifetime, Mu'in-ud-Din Chishti preached that the best form of prayers included: listening to the grievances of the suffering people; helping the needy; and feeding the hungry. The Khwaja would also say that people with the following three characteristics could legitimately be considered as friends of God: river like generosity; affection like that of sun; and modesty and hospitality of earth. None of them discriminate in what they have to offer. Not for nothing people from all walks of life and above narrow religious and political boundaries continue to flock to his *dargah* for 800 years now, and even when there may be so much distaste for political violence in the name of Islam.

Complete submission to the will of their beloved God helped Sufis combat adversities – social, economic or natural. In a miracle story attributed to the Khwaja as early as the middle of the fourteenth century, it was reported that a Sultanate official, Malik Ikhtiyar-ud-Din Aibak, went to meet Mu'in-ud-Din Chishti and offered a cash grant, which the Sufi Sheikh refused to accept. Malik Ikhtiyar-ud-Din was shocked to see that the Baba was sitting on a carpet, under which a whole canal of gold coins was flowing! He was told to take away his *nazrana* (gift) which had no value for the Khwaja.

In the above anecdote, there were several considerations, which were hedged through a miracle (*karamat*), a typical trope in Sufi practices: first, questions regarding *halal/haram* nature of Ikhtiyar-ud-Din's income; second, medieval *muftis* and *muhtasibs*, conscience-keepers of the time, were much more ruthless than the modern-day income tax commissioners; third, Sufis took pride in their poverty than being embarrassed by their new-found richness; fourth, the Sufi may not be sure whether his family of several sons would be able to handle this, gracefully.

In a similar incident, one of the Khwaja's spiritual successors, Hamid-ud-Din, who had settled down in nearby Nagaur, rejected a huge cash grant from another Sultanate official. Before doing so, Hamid-ud-Din had consulted his wife and the venerable lady confirmed her Sufi-husband's apprehensions by saying they were happy, despite their poverty, which they were able to handle through cultivation of a small portion of land and spinning a few yards of clothes – both were sufficient for their creature comfort.

Sufis were sharply critical of the hypocrises, especially involving religious rituals. For them, natural calamities like earthquakes and plague and terror-attacks of the kind led by Changez Khan in the thirteenth century (who by the way was not a Muslim) were punishments sent from above for the wretchedness of the men on earth. In such situations, when people would rush seeking help from Sufis they would be told it was too late to intervene and save them from the disaster. They should run for their lives, praying to God for help, and prayers may not work either for people's *niyat* was not good and that is why the punishment.

This was summed up in a Persian quartet (*ruba'i*) quoted by another famous medieval Chishti Sufi master, Hazrat Nizam-ud-Din Auliya:

Giram ke namazhai bisyar kuni
Wa-z-rozai dahar beshumar kuni

Ta dil na kuni ze ghussai wa kine tahi
Sad man gul bar sare yak khar kuni

(Agreed that you perform a lot of *namaz*
And also keep fast for many days
Yet if your heart isn't cleansed off anger and hatred
It's like dumping a hundred mounds of flowers on top of a thorn.)

Speaking in such a critical language for the need for reform within and just a little bit of humanism or compassion, Mu'in-ud-Din and a series of his successors – Qutb-ud-Din Bakhtiyar Kaki (shrine at Mehrauli, south Delhi), Farid-ud-Din Ganj-i-Shakar, more popularly known as Baba Farid (buried at Pak Patan, Ajodhan, in Punjab, now in Pakistan), Nizam-ud-Din Auliya (*dargah* in central Delhi) and Nasir-ud-Din Chiragh Dilli (tomb in south Delhi) – created a whole sacred geography of Islam in the Indian subcontinent, with the successors and disciples of each of these saints spreading and creating a network of popular piety that has stood the test of time for centuries together.

This practice of spiritually-oriented Islam is in sharp contrast to political Islam which thrives on violence and terror, despite the fact that Islam is supposed to be a religion of peace. Sufi saints have shown, through their practice, that this claim of peace with all is not an empty rhetoric. This is despite the fact that Sufi traditions have not shied from claiming that Islam has spread in large parts of the subcontinent through the blessed presence of early Sufi masters. Small Muslim communities emerged wherever Sufis settled down.

Mid-fourteenth century Sufi literature presents Mu'in-ud-Din Chishti as an Islamiser, whose arrival at Ajmer was resented by Prithviraj Chauhan. By late-fifteenth and early-sixteenth century, the *dargah* was attracting a large number of devotees, who offered flowers and *chadars* and prayed for their well-being – *mannats* of different kinds. Many of these devotees were not Muslims, but had faith in the miraculous powers of the saint. The charismatic appeal of the saint and his shrine was fully established in the sacred geography of Hindustan by the time of the Mughal emperor Akbar, in the latter half of the sixteenth century. However, Sufi texts were already referring to Mu'in-ud-Din Chishti as Sultan-ul-Hind from mid-fourteenth century onwards. Thus, this image of Mu'in-ud-Din as the patron saint of Hindustan has a long history.

The Chishtis wanted to steer clear of politics, and yet would be viewed as important sources of legitimacy for political regimes – both because of their large followers and miraculous powers they reportedly enjoyed. In his own time, Mu'in-ud-Din Chishti interacted with the Delhi Sultan Shams-ud-Din Iltutmish, and on his request let his successor in the Chishti *silsila*, Qutb-ud-Din Bakhtiyar Kaki, stay in Delhi and bless the capital city with his presence. Mu'in-ud-Din himself preferred to live in Ajmer, which he believed was the command to him by Prophet Muhammad as received in a dream. Mu'in-ud-Din was from Sistan in Iran, he saw the dream in Baghdad in Iraq and, thus, came to settle down in India. Ajmer in Rajasthan was going to be his blessed home, transforming it as a major centre of Sufi pilgrimage. The Chishti *silsila* itself started in Chisht in Afghanistan of the good old medieval period. Sufi exemplars associated with the *silsila* travelled far and wide with their message of peace, love and tolerance, which remained their defining characteristics in the past and continues in the present.

10

THE MAKING OF THE QUTB MINAR COMPLEX AND ITS HISTORICAL SIGNIFICANCE

THE TURKISH FORCES of Shahab-ud-Din Muhammad Ghori, led by Qutb-ud-Din Aibak, had captured Delhi (*c.*1193) without much resistance and set about eliminating the symbols of Rajput power and prestige. Some temples were demolished in the wake of the conquest. Their debris was utilized to construct a congregational mosque (Jama Masjid) at Lal Kot. It was later called Quwwatul Islam or Qubbatul Islam mosque, highlighting the might or stronghold of Islam. Remarkably, there was no mutilation of the bodies of the dead in the battlefields, no general massacre of the populace, and no major demographic dislocation. Much as the chroniclers like Minhaj-us-Siraj celebrated the conquest of new territories, the conquerors themselves preferred minimum use of force. Though iconoclasm may have played a role, places of worship were generally plundered for their wealth. Alternatively, their destruction was aimed at hammering home the point that the old regime was overthrown. It could no longer protect the people and their religious places.

In the event of the Turkish conquest of Delhi, people were supposed to know that the Turks and their sultan had established a new, Islamic order. Indeed, the minaret attached to Delhi's congregational mosque, known as the Qutb Minar, was later perceived as a victory tower (*vijayastambha*). Whether the call of the *muezzin* (crier) for prayer was heard by all the people or not, the 72.50 metre high Minar testified to the visual enunciation of Muslim power. The adjoining structures of the Qutb complex, including the mosque, the tombs of Sultan Shams-ud-Din Iltutmish and Imam Zamin, and the additions by Sultan Ala-ud-Din Khalji (Alai Darwaza, Alai Madrasa and Alai Minar), together constitute a rich source of the architecture of the emerging Delhi Sultanate. The borrowings, adaptations and synthesis, which went into the construction of these buildings – both in terms of material and design – paved the way for the growth and development of a marvellous Indo-Muslim architecture in the subsequent period.

It will be interesting to explore the process of the construction of these buildings at the Qutb complex, narrate stories and anecdotes connected to them – whether oral or found in the written sources – take account of their renovation and upkeep over time, and point to the danger to their very existence and contestations over their identity in the wake of a threatening political ecology. Mention may be made here of the possibility of the pre-Muslim existence of the minaret, though secularists will be loath to discuss this, the site being on the hit-list of Hindu communalists.

However, it will be unfair to ignore an important observation of Sir Syed Ahmad Khan in his authoritative mid-nineteenth-century text, *Asar-us-Sanadid* (Urdu Academy, Delhi, 2000 edn., pp. 166–7), that not only the mosque was built on the site where the temple constructed by Prithviraja

Chauhan existed before the Muslim conquest, but the first story of the Minar was also a part of it. In any case, the 7.20 metre iron pillar, reportedly installed at Lal Kot by the Tomar king Anangpal stood in the courtyard (*sehan*) of the Qubbat-ul-Islam mosque, the erstwhile site of Lal Kot. Apart from being an object of curiosity, the pillar, said to be a standard (*dhvaja*) of Vishnu from the Gupta period, probably served as a reminder of the conquering power of Islam under the Delhi Sultans. The mutilated figures of Hindu deities on the walls and pillars around the courtyard add to such an image. Beyond modern questions of secularism and communalism, defacement of the deities and desecration of the places of worship of the conquered point to manifestations of the visual culture of violence, legitimizing a new political order in the medieval period, even as the general population was not ordered to follow the religion of the victors.

Indeed, in their misplaced understanding of the Sultanate as an Islamic state, the *ulama* (Muslim religious scholars) wanted Sultan Shams-ud-Din Iltutmish (who ruled 1211-36) to confront the Hindus of the capital city (*dar-ul-khilafa*) of Delhi. In a measure which speaks of the Sultan's attempts for rapprochement with non-Muslims, Iltutmish rejected the *ulama*'s demand. The Turks had realised that it was difficult to rule a vast non-Muslim population through strict adherence to a narrow interpretation of the Shariat or Islamic law as interpreted by jurists belonging to the Hanafi school. Instead, they evolved a broad, almost secular state law (*zawabit-i-mulki*) with public protestation of respect to Muslim divines and their institutions, later articulated in the *Fatawa-i-Jahandari* by Ziya-ud-Din Barani, an influential noble and prominent disciple of the Chishti saint Nizam-ud-Din Auliya.

The Muslim population of the city was, however, already increasing rapidly in the early decades of the thirteenth century. Significantly enough, the enthronement of Qutb-ud-Din Aibak (who ruled 1206-10) coincided with the election of Ghenghis Khan (who should not be mistaken as a Muslim) as the great leader of the Mongol hordes. The advent of the Mongols led to large-scale devastation in Central and West Asia in the next 50 years. Major centres of Islam like Bukhara and Baghdad were sacked. Delhi was the only place where Muslims could escape the wrath of the Tartars. Islam prospered in Delhi with the name of the Caliph still being mentioned in the Friday sermons (*khutba*) and on coins (*sikka*). A number of Sufi saints also came to settle in Delhi. The Qutb complex and the fast expanding Mehrauli area constituted a conspicuous intersection of political and sacred geography of the city. No wonder, in course of time the capital acquired the venerable epithet of 'Hazrat-i-Dehli'!

The rulers disliked the arrogance of the *ulama* and felt that the Sufis' position on such question as relation with Hindus, and generally on matters related to Shariat, was more appropriate. Delhi was, thus, going to have a multicultural and multireligious complexion. Controversial religious issues, which had the potential to break the pluralistic fabric of the city, did come to the public arena occasionally, but in the end sanity and a basic respect for pluralism prevailed.

[Extracted from Raziuddin Aquil, 'Hazrat-i-Dehli: The Making of the Chishti Sufi Centre and the Stronghold of Islam', *South Asia Research*, vol. 28(1), 2008, pp. 23-48. Also see, Raziuddin Aquil, 'Hazrat-i-Dehli: Chishti Sufism and the Making of the Cosmopolitan Character of the City of Dehli', in Supriya Chaudhuri (ed.) *Religion and the City in India*, London and New York: Routledge, 2022, pp. 48-61.]

11

MAHBUB-I ILAHI HAZRAT KHWAJA NIZAM-UD-DIN AULIYA

CHISHTI SUFI SAINT Hazrat Khwaja Nizam-ud-Din Auliya (d. 1325) was a living legend of his time in Delhi in the late-thirteenth and early-fourteenth centuries. Nizam-ud-din had continued the chain, order or *silsila* of Chishti Sufi *shaikh*s as the foremost disciple of Khwaja Farid-ud-Din Ganj-i-Shakar (d. 1265), popularly known as Shaikh Farid or Baba Farid, who was a much respected *guru*-like figure in Punjab's shared cultural tradition. The Sultans and their associates enjoyed enormous political power during the period and some even tried to create difficulties for Nizam-ud-Din Auliya. Their boorish behaviour was mostly forgiven and consigned to the forgettable past, whereas reports of both horrendous violence and good governance have survived in Sufi circles and through them in popular memories and historical records. There is lesson here for all concerned: while the charisma of Hazrat Nizam-ud-Din has survived for over seven centuries, no one is really bothered where a Khalji or Tughlaq might be lying buried–often in the debris of their own making.

Like his tomb (*dargah*) in Delhi today, a large number of devotees – both poor souls and power elite – thronged Nizam-ud-Din's *jama'at-khana* (hospice). Though he wanted to steer clear off the reigning Sultans, he allowed a number of leading courtiers, members of ruling families and even some crooks to become his disciples – hoping to make some change in their heart so that they learn to respect other beings. Histories of violent past have shown how men in power abuse and bodily mutilate those who do not have any capacity to even resist them. Forcing someone to eat human excreta, vegetarian food, or even a *chapati*, for that matter, is not such a big crime in the annals of history. Mercifully, there have also been people who have advocated sanity and basic human dignity, cutting across institutional boundaries of religions.

Hazrat Nizam-ud-Din's prominent disciples Amir Khusrau (father of classical Hindustani musical traditions) and Ziya-ud-Din Barani (historian and political ideologue) have portrayed him in glorious terms, and his own *malfuzat* (conversations and teachings) have been put together in a volume called *Fawa'id-ul-Fu'ad* (Benefiting the Heart) by another disciple, nobleman and poet, Amir Hasan Sijzi. Checked and corrected by Nizam-ud-Din himself, the text is a must-read for anyone wishing to learn how to lead a civilized human life in a world otherwise full of violations of different kinds. One chapter recording the discussion in the hospice on a blessed Thursday of the holy-month of Ramazan illustrates how to deal with the tricky issue of converting non-Muslims to Islam and whether it was worth it.

It is recorded in *Fawa'id-ul-Fu'ad* that a disciple arrived in the middle of a discussion, along with a Hindu whom he addressed as his brother. When both were seated, Nizam-ud-Din asked the disciple whether the said brother of his had any interest in Islam. The disciple replied that it was precisely for that very purpose that he had brought him to his feet so that by the blessing of his glance he might become a Muslim. With tears in his eyes, the Sufi Shaikh remarked that force or persuasion cannot change anyone's heart, though purification of the soul and spiritual satisfaction was possible through the grace of the company of a devout Muslim.

In this context, Nizam-ud-Din narrated the story of conversion of the king of Iraq who was entrusted by second Caliph Umar to the company of a pious Muslim. The dethroned king had earlier refused to embrace Islam even under the threat of execution, but the company of the virtuous Muslim made such an impact on him that he subsequently returned to the Caliph and professed his faith in Islam. The former king also reminded the new Caliph that he alone will be responsible for the destruction of an otherwise prosperous country of Iraq. Further, Nizam-ud-Din also commented on the dichotomy of moral integrity of Islam and Muslims through the story of a Jew who stayed in the neighbourhood of a first generation Iranian Sufi master, Bayazid Bustami. When Bayazid passed away, the Jew was asked by some persons as to why he did not become a Muslim at the hands of the Shaikh. The Jew retorted as to what kind of Muslim they wanted him to become, adding that if Islam was what Bayazid practised he would not be able to attain it and if it were the way Muslims lived he was sick of it.

The above observations, read together with other anecdotes of conversion recounted by Nizam-ud-Din, clearly show that he was not altogether disinterested in proselytization. He, indeed, believed that conversion was possible through gradual cultural transformation or through occasional cataclysmic change of heart. More importantly, though some fanatical antagonists could have accused Nizam-ud-Din of missing the opportunity to convert that non-Muslim visitor, for the Chishti master reform within was the best means for the propagation of the faith. A good Muslim should be a fine human being, and he should be continuously searching his own soul.

[Earlier version of the article was published in the *Sunday Guardian*: http://www.sunday-guardian.com/analysis/nizamuddin-is-revered-not-khalji-or-tughlaq.]

12

DAYS IN THE LIFE OF A SUFI

SUFISM IS A vibrant spiritual movement within Islam. It has several strands which have developed across centuries and in different parts of the world. Originating in eighth century Iraq with precedents even earlier in the times of Prophet Muhammad himself, Sufi traditions grew as part of a powerful mystical movement and spread to all corners of the known world. Central to this is the complete, even obsessive, love and devotion for God and to achieve a blissful mystical union with Him. This they called *ishq-i haqiqi* (true love for God), compared to *ishq-i majazi* (desire for this-worldly objects of love). They aspired to achieve this through a systematic cultivation of the soul, purifying the lower-self, and dedicating themselves in the service of all the creations of God. Service to humanity was considered the best form of worship. This was done through charitable endeavours, blessings and benediction for which large numbers of people throng to Sufi shrines, *mazar*s and *dargah*s even today. Many of the visitors and devotees to these places are not Muslims, but they have faith in the spiritual powers of Sufi saints. It is believed by the visitors that the Sufis have achieved nearness to God. This belief prevails even in times when Islam is stigmatized because of terror and violence in its name. This means that the followers understand the distinction between the humanism of Sufi spirituality and brutalities involved in violent political abuses of Islam.

Sufis also adopted spiritual practices which were beyond the juridically recommended Islamic obligations. This would often run them into trouble with the custodians of Islam. Sufis defended themselves as true followers of the path of the Prophet in their complete and unconditional submission to the will of God. They expressed these through their voluminous writings, discourses and powerful poetry. The latter included a systematically developed art form – often blending song, music and dance, which also appealed to popular taste and catered to the need for some music in one's life. Sufis recognized that only a heartless being will have no sense of music.

Wherever Sufis went they got themselves embedded in local culture and spoke of their love for God in the language the people understood. In the subcontinent, from as early as the eleventh century onward, they sang and preached in Punjabi in Punjab, Dakkani in Deccan, Bengali in Bengal. In the cow-belt of Hindustan, they spoke in Hindi and from the fifteenth century onward avoided eating beef in deference to the sentiments of sections of people. They also composed their poetry of love in a genre called *premakhyan*, the best example of which is *Padmavat* of Malik Muhammad Jaysi. This latter text was in the news in recent times, as a Hindi film based on it could not handle the intricate entanglements of literature, spirituality and politics in history and the present leading to a caricature of the original poetry. In the charged political, atmosphere, looking at Sufi *premakhyan* texts, cynics may wonder how is it that Sufis wrote such exquisite poetry of love despite being Muslims, especially as the latter are increasingly and erroneously being identified as terrorists or their sympathizers.

The stories of miracles and other anecdotes in Sufi texts frequently relate to a Sufi Shaikh flying on a camel-back to Mecca for Hajj, the holy Ka'ba coming over to India for circumambulation around the blessed personality of a Sufi Shaikh and his spiritually soaked hospice, walls floating in the air at the command of a Sufi, rivers getting dried up to let the Sufi Shaikh cross, a river of molten silver flowing underneath the prayer carpet of the saint, soil, stone, firewood transformed into gold, revival of the dead, many cases of spiritual healing for which the people would crowd hospices and shrines, ability to see distant places and to foresee the good and the evil in future, and the details of the effects of *jalal* (curse on the opponents) and *jamal* (grace and favour), on those who had faith in him. These anecdotes, with all their spectacular and paranormal contents, can be identified as pertaining to the domain of prediction and divination, encounters with opponents and the competitive nature of popular spirituality, conversion of the opponent and others as disciples with or without direct and immediate acceptance of Islam, and Sufi miracles as benevolence through help in distress and healing practices.

Many of the miraculous stories are recurring, repetitive and common to diverse traditions, and therefore their historicity and truthfulness as historical facts will be difficult to establish. Yet, it is easy to see, from the texts in which they have been included, the relevance, popularity, and contexts in which such stories emerged and spread through the subcontinent. Many of the stories were narrated by none other than Hazrat Nizam-ud-Din Auliya in his own lifetime, and many others were recounted by his disciple and successor in the Chishti *silsila*, Khwaja Nasir-ud-Din Chiragh Dilli. These stories, therefore, cannot be dismissed as unimportant for understanding the relevance of Sufism and its popular appeal. Supernatural feats are indeed the Sufi saints' sources of authority in the public domain. It is only for those miraculous interventions that a large majority of visitors continue to throng Sufi *dargah*s and *mazar*s even in modern times when there is great difficulty in community relations involving Muslims and others. The majority of visitors to shrines are still non-Muslims, for they understand the distinction between the spiritual language of love of Sufis for God and the violent nature of politics in our times, and perhaps also in the past. So while many people visit Nizam-ud-Din Dargah every day, few would be interested in knowing where the Tughlaq Sultan was buried.

Popularity of a Sufi saint depended upon how successfully he demonstrated his miraculous power. The people appropriated a miracle-working Sufi Shaikh, expected him to stay in their neighbourhood and perform miracles for them. This is a role the Sufis continue to perform even after they pass away, because it is believed that saints never die. Lying in their graves, they continue to look after their disciples and followers. Visitors to their *mazar*s and *dargah*s are thus blessed with the surrounding spirituality and charisma. This has made Sufi shrines relevant for all times, in the past and the present. Spiritually soaked Thursday evenings at the *dargah* and the occasion of annual *urs* (death anniversary of Sufis) are considered to be especially rewarding. The shrines are open to everyone: man-woman, high-low, rich-poor,

Hindu-Muslim, Sikh-Christian. None are discriminated against, for all are creations of God, and Sufis considered themselves as friends and lovers of God. The stories recounted above bring out this and several other significant dimensions which together make Sufism a vibrant spiritual movement within Islam, with a history going back twelve centuries and counting. It was part of the great traditions of Islam at their zenith and it is also witness to the contemporary history of Islam at its lowest ebb. In either case, its relevance is a matter of hope and solace for those who seek to live in a world promising peace and harmonious coexistence of all the beautiful creations of God. For, it creates a spiritually imbued brotherhood of unity in diversity.

[Excerpted from *Days in the Life of a Sufi: 101 Enchanting Stories of Wisdom* by Raziuddin Aquil, published by Pan Macmillan India. Also published in the *National Herald*, 1 November 2020.]

13

THE HISTORIC PROJECTS OF SULTAN MUHAMMAD TUGHLAQ

FOURTEENTH-CENTURY Delhi Sultan Muhammad bin Tughlaq's outrageous *farmans* (orders) are invoked every time people in power come up with out of the box ideas, drastically changing the system and adversely affecting the general populace. The Sultan's eventful rule for nearly 26 years, 1325-51 CE, offers important insights on how brutal measures adopted to implement even some very good ideas can get completely discredited. The people rebelled against the despot because of the severity of his actions; and the latter severely punished those who defied his authority – the more the people resisted, the more they were chastized.

At the height of his power, Muhammad Tughlaq presided over a large subcontinental empire. Condemned as somewhat mad or devilish, the charges levelled against him include: the all-knowing Sultan would not listen to any advice, no matter how good and well-meaning; he would not brook any criticism even from people who were not opposed to him; he would not tolerate any opposition and the opponents could be suppressed and removed in most ingenious ways; he had no qualms in killing his own father to capture power, though no judge could have proved the charge; finally, it was his grand ambition that goaded him to go for some outlandish projects which proved to be his undoing, both because he was thinking ahead of his time and trying to emerge as a world-conqueror.

Having subdued the whole of India, the monarch wanted to conquer the Himalayas – the entire mountainous region between India and China. This would enable him to further break into Central Asia, conquering Khurasan and going as far as Iran and Iraq. A huge amount of money was spent in mobilizing the army, but the project proved to be a damp squib. Hill chiefs who controlled the territories now falling under Himachal and Kashmir, foxed Delhi army into a veritable death-trap; lakhs of horsemen were deployed and only a few returned to the capital to break the news of the massacre.

The money for the disastrous campaign was collected through two related measures: implementation of a heavy tax regime and introduction of token currency of brass and copper, instead of usual gold and silver. Both hard-working agriculturalists and cautious traders were badly hit by the move. A couple of years of poor monsoon further aggravated the crisis, with famine raging and scarcity of food and fodder causing starvation and death. Minting and circulation of a large quantum of fake copper coins also adversely affected trade and commerce, even as the king was mocked as hungry for gold. Waking up to the reality of a dwindling economy, the ruler offered loans and subsidy (*taqavi*) to hapless peasants and also announced that copper coins, fake or otherwise, could be exchanged with gold and silver *tankas*, but much damage had already been done. Though China was showing the way, time for paper currency or plastic cards had not come yet.

The failures of these schemes meant widespread unrest. The somewhat neglected southern India demanded special attention, which the king thought could be tackled better from the formidable fort of Devgiri – renamed Daulatabad and announced as new capital. Accordingly, Delhi's power elite was ordered to be relocated – causing much anxiety and hardship to those affected. The ruler even used his own mother setting example by undertaking the arduous journey to prove the seriousness of the project. Like other schemes, this did not work either. Delhi's power was considerably diminished, even as the despot could not hold on to his control over Tamil country; soon, Kannada and Telugu-speaking regions were usurped by emerging Vijayanagara empire and north-western Deccan saw the rise of Bahmani kingdom. By the end of his rule, the Sultan also witnessed revolts in Maharashtra and Gujarat – his last bastions. Meanwhile, Bengal had already gone its own distinct way.

Through all this, Muhammad Tughlaq continued to placate religious leaders, philosophers, foreign dignitaries and hitherto marginalized wannabes, besides seeking testimonials from the Caliph in Egypt. When disgusted, he even contemplated vacating his seat and going on a pilgrimage, but he was not the one to give up easily. Disobedience to the autocrat was interpreted as defiance of the authority of God, which demanded severe chastizement. Therefore, instead of focusing on policy and governance, he applied himself excessively to the business of punishment; none could escape his wrath – treatment ranging from simple beheading to more spectacular skinning and cutting into pieces to make veritable meat-*pulao* for serving to elephants, who were expected to revolt in disgust, for elephants were supposed to be vegetarians.

Eventually, as a reliable courtier reported: in his death amidst widespread violence, both the ruthless Sultan and the haggard public got rid of each other.

[Recommended readings: *Tarikh-i-Firuzshahi* of Ziya-ud-Din Barani, *Futuh-us-Salatin* of Izz-ud-Din Isami, and *Rehla* of Ibn Battuta.]

14

INDO-PERSIAN HISTORIOGRAPHY: ZIYA-UD-DIN BARANI AND HIS *TARIKH-I FIRUZSHAHI*

ZIYA-UD-DIN BARANI'S mid-fourteenth century *Tarikh-i Firuzshahi* is one of the finest examples of Indo-Persian historiography, a text much abused in modern times by colonial authors, Hindu nationalists and other interested parties. Barani himself is dismissed in secular histories as a bigoted theologian whose views smacked of communalism. Such an understanding of the author sounds simplistic, even contradictory – dismissing as unimportant the work of a fine historian, perceptive political theorist, well-informed personal advisor of Sultan Muhammad Tughlaq, sincere disciple of Chishti Sufi Nizam-ud-Din Auliya, and close friends with poet Amir Khusrau.

Indeed, Barani had nothing to do with theology and he dismissed as impracticable the claims of Shariat as state law, advocated by the Sunnite *ulama*. Instead, the author was articulating an elitist power discourse: the supremacy and domination of Islam can only be established in contrast to the inferiority and subordination of non-Islam, since power cannot be enjoyed in a vacuum. Conversion to Islam is not recommended in such an ideology and even Indian converts to Islam were to be treated as inferior people who should not have been converted in the first place.

History is written by the conquerors sometimes on the body of those they decimate, but the conquered people often survive to write their own histories. With a certain degree of democratization of the Sultanate polity, a large number of Indians were able to break into the system to change the course of history. The gradual political and social change had meant that one did not even need to formally convert to Islam to rise in the Sultanate nobility and bureaucracy; a process initiated as much by the emergence of the Khalji and Tughlaq Sultans as by the presence of the Chishtis with their inclusive cultural practices. These new people were giving a tough time to Delhi's power elite, previously entrenched in the system. Certainly, Barani demeans himself by condemning them using a variety of invectives: unworthy, ignoble, low-born and bazaar people can have no sense of history!

Misfit in the changing scheme of things and sidelined from the court of Firuz Shah Tughlaq, Barani refashioned himself to start his career as a historian at the age of about 70 years, realizing all along how the times had changed from a strong Ghiyas-ud-Din Balban's sophisticated violence to consolidate his position to a ruthless Muhammad Tughlaq who built an empire geographically comparable to those of the Mauryas; it was another matter that the Tughlaq Sultan could not control and govern that empire to anyone's satisfaction. And, as Barani perceptively put it: the Sultan's death meant both he and the subject people got rid of each other!

In the Introduction to the *Tarikh-i Firuzshahi*, which is now available in a reliable English translation by Ishtiyaq

Ahmad Zilli (Primus Books, New Delhi, 2015), Barani has emphasized the value of acquiring historical knowledge, outlined his method, and stressed what he has written is a matter of truth, arguing his work can be read as a chronicle of the rule of the Sultans, covering nearly a century, or as political analysis of regulations regarding matters of governance, or as counsels and advice for rulers – historical insights as guiding principles in the politics of the present.

According to Barani, historians should be able to rise above the limitations of fear or favour in discussing virtues and merits of those in power, not sweeping under the carpet their failings, demerits and cruelties either. If it was not possible to openly criticize a despot, historians could deploy their linguistic skills in such a way that they were able to speak by means of allusion or euphemism; and, if historians found it altogether impossible to write about a contemporary ruler, they could be excused, but as regards people of the past they were expected to write truth alone. For, any rubbish could be easily trashed and such books were frequently guttered for the paper to be recycled for writing afresh; for Barani, that was often the case with people of low origin peddling falsehood as truth, betraying ambitions for something they did not deserve.

Modern academic institutions and the discipline of history remain awfully elitist, but mercifully no historian worth his craft can now flaunt his prejudices in such a crude manner, certainly not those who aspire for a place in the history of historiography. Typically known for his aggressive intent, Barani has concluded his Introduction with a claim only he could make:

Gar be-guyam ke nist dar aalam
Masal tarikh-i mun kitab-i digar
Chun dar-in ilm aalimi nabud
Ke kunad gufta-i maara baawar

(If I say there does not exist in the world
Any other book like the history of mine
Since there is none who is proficient in this subject
Who will believe in what I am saying.)

[Earlier published in the *Sunday Guardian*: https://www.sundayguardianlive.com/opinion/1200-history-written-conquerors.]

15

CULTURAL DYNAMICS AS HERITAGE

A VARIETY OF CULTURAL practices, intellectual traditions, religious contestations as well as questions of political patronage and abuse shape the cultural dynamics of medieval and early modern India. Our cultural heritage can be preserved to sustain pluralistic diversity that has come down to modern times. On the other hand, the significant cultural markers, including built heritage, can also be dismantled to create a society that is awfully ignorant of its own past. Some of the prominent features of crucial significance to the understanding of the cultural history of pre-modern India may be highlighted here.

1. *Religious movements:* Medieval and early modern Sufi-Bhakti complex preached peaceful coexistence and tolerance of other people's religious beliefs and practices, which explains the amazing diversity we have inherited. In understanding these religious and cultural processes, we need to also take cognisance of cases of aggressive sectarianism, complex identity formation, questions of conversion and occasional attempts to abuse political power.
2. *Literary traditions:* Some accomplished historians have begun to survey a variety of literature in many

languages across time and space. These include classical languages as well as a number of regional vernaculars, though in many cases the boundaries between classical and vernacularity as well as forms and genres collapse. Together, they reveal interesting ways in which literary works were produced, and show how authors and reading publics resorted to inter-textual cross-referencing. They also indicate the direction the emerging new literary histories can take for a more fruitful understanding of India's vast literary traditions, especially how its past has shaped the present.

3. *Music and dance forms:* Art forms included expertise and excellence developed in wide-ranging fields of poetry, music and dance. Some people remain caught in misplaced belief in the myth of music being forbidden in Islam, whereas the evidence to the contrary abounds, both in theory and practice. Sufi hospices and royal courts have played significant role in the development of these art forms which must be properly recognized. Ghazal and *qawwali* come to mind, as does kathak.
4. *Festivities and little pleasures of life:* With historians now working with a whole range of source material, it is possible to write interesting new history of food habits, consumption, bazaars and *mela*s, as well as gender and bodily practices. Literary works of poets like Jafar Zatalli and Nazir Akbarabadi can help us understand questions related to gender, besides speaking truth to power and celebrating multiple idioms of politics and culture.

5. *Visual cultures:* Pre-colonial rulers especially expressed grandeur and expressions of their power and sovereignty in architecture and paintings they sponsored. In this context, critical question of desecration of places of worship also comes to mind, which should not be hushed under the carpet, nor should they be abused in modern times for narrow political gains as we are now faced with in some cases. One can derive lessons from the past; attempting to take revenge for historical wrongs, genuine or imagined, tantamounts to harakiri in society.
6. *Political patronage:* Pre-colonial India witnessed broad and inclusive framework of political ideas, theories and practices adopted by emperors like Akbar. By contrast, rulers like Aurangzeb drew on narrow sectarian ideologies, especially invoking the name of Sunni Islam for legitimizing some of his outrageous political aggrandizement. Violence was possible in the wake of conquests and empire-building, but medieval works on political theory advocated minimum use of force under all circumstances.

Thus, historically, cultural diversity epitomises our civilizational character. On the other hand, destructive pulls of communalism and bigotry continue to hurt the society fairly badly. However, for all we know, sanity prevails in the long run. Some key historical texts show enough light. They include many interesting versions of *Ramayana* and *Mahabharata* in Sanskrit and vernaculars; *Adi Granth*, or *Guru Granth Sahib*, which comprises devotional compositions of not only Sikh *gurus*, but also of such iconoclasts as Sant Kabir and Punjabi Chishti Sufi, Shaikh Farid; *Padmavat* of Malik Muhammad Jaysi, which was in the news in recent past, is a fine example of Sufi poetry of love in Hindi in a genre called the *premakhyan*; *Ramcharitmanas* of Tulsidas, a powerful expression of Rama-bhakti in Mughal India; and *Akbarnama* and *Ain-i Akbari* of Abu'l Fazl, articulating Mughal political ideology on how to govern a vast subcontinental country with so much diversity, especially for resolving the question of religious assertions through emphasis on broad-based governing principles, conceptualized as peace with all. Together, they showcase what we cherish as the best in India's inclusive political culture, devotional practices showing the way for peaceful coexistence, and remarkable achievements in the cultural arena, whether in the excellence in literary practices or in exquisite examples of the built heritage.

[Based on a lecture by the author at Amity University, Noida. Published in the *Sunday Guardian*: https://www.sundayguardian live.com/opinion/cultural-dynamics-heritage.]

16

KABIR AND THE IDEA OF UNITY IN DIVERSITY IN BHAKTI TRADITIONS

IT IS IMPORTANT to take cognizance of, even celebrate, the extraordinary life and legends of Sant Kabir (d. 1518) for his continuing relevance to questions of communal harmony and social justice, which are often marred by aggressive religious contestations and political violence. As a syncretic figure, with possible Brahmin antecedents and an abandoned child brought up in a Muslim weaver's family, Kabir is well-known as a *bhakti*-sant of iconoclastic ideas challenging social hierarchies and religious hypocrises in the political context of the Lodi-Afghan rule in north India. His teachings called for peaceful coexistence of different religious groups.

Several strands of medieval *bhakti* movements, led by devotional poets and reformers from marginal sections of society condemned religious rituals, criticized caste or *jati*-based hierarchies and discrimination and advocated the need to discover Rama, a formless God, inside one's heart. Some traditions of *bhakti* also styled themselves as Hindu religious movements, revolving around Sri Rama of Ayodhya. Though religious leaders such as Sant Kabir and Guru Nanak defied contentious political boundaries of Islam and Hinduism, religious fields witnessed violent formations of communities.

The *sants* and *gurus* competed with each other, appropriated mystical and social ideas and attracted followers. In most cases, the latter went on to organize themselves as distinct communities or sects (*panths* and *sampradays*). In many cases, the followers completely transformed the original teachings of their spiritual *gurus*. The communities formed around them often sought to use political power to humble and subdue each other.

Preaching in latter half of fifteenth and early decades of sixteenth centuries, Kabir sharply criticized not only Hindu and Muslim religious leaders, but also found faults with self-styled Sufis and *yogis*. It is important to reiterate here that Kabir criticized the ritual of animal sacrifice among Hindus, but he also reserved his trenchant critique for condemnation of slaughter of animals by Muslims. A long poem in the well-known compilation of his compositions, the *Bijak*, which has been studied by a number of reputed scholars of *bhakti* traditions, attacks Muslim preference for non-vegetarian food in the context of an aggressive vegetarianism, particularly against cow-slaughter, emerging in the politically volatile fifteenth-sixteenth centuries. Speaking in support of vegetarianism, Kabir countered, whose *farman* it was to kill goats and chicken to consume them. Making it more explicit, he mocks at the alleged fake propriety and religiosity of Muslims by pointing out that they fast during the day and eat beef at night.

For *yogis*, Kabir's advice was that spiritual practices like *pranayama* and other forms of meditations are of no use till the heart of the person concerned was not cleansed and Rama discovered within. Exhorting the people to have a *darshan* of the Lord in the mirror of one's own heart, Kabir advised in a verse compiled in a *Granthavali*, that the mirror needed continuous cleaning of the filth gathered on it:

Jau darsan dekhya chahiye, tau darpan manjat rahiye |
Jab darpan laage kaayi, tab darsan kiya na jaayi | |

Kabir's attack on Muslim religious leaders (*ulama* and *qazi*s, not sparing Sufis either) and also *yogi*s would make him an interesting case for appropriation in Vaishnavite-Brahmanical *sagun* tradition of medieval Rama *bhakti*. On the other hand, his non-Brahmanical Hindu followers, the Kabir-panthis, believed in the *nirgun* (formless) God. Beginning as a Sufi disciple of Shaikh Taqi of Kara-Manikpur (later Allahabad), Kabir himself crossed all boundaries. In doing so, he was searching for common ground as *yogi*s and Sufis also had done. Gorakhnath is known to have taken a position closer to Sufis, referring to them as belonging to the caste (*jati*) of Allah, for they knew the door of the house of the Lord. Similarly, Kabir's contemporary Sufis, who believed in the concept of *wahdat-ul-wujud* (monism or unity of existence), appropriated Yogic ideas and practices presented in a text called *Amritkund*, the Arabic and Persian translations of which were much in demand in Sufi circles of medieval India. One of the enthusiasts was a leading Chishti Sufi, Abdul Quddus Gangohi, who accessed this text from his strong position as a responsible Muslim religious leader and found no contradiction in styling himself as Alakhdas in his own mystical poetry in Hindi. He would even conflate distinctions to say that there was no difference between the notions of monistic *wahdat-ul-wujud* (which sections of Sufis found similar to *advaita*) and monotheistic *tauhid* (one God emphasized by the *ulama*).

Indeed, in the Sufi-*bhakti* complex of medieval India, the formless God was called by a variety of names (Allah, Rama, Rahim, Khuda or Alakh Niranjan). Kabir's own search for common ground through the unity of God (*wahdat-ul-wujud*, and not necessarily *tauhid*) can be seen in his claim of the possibility of complete assimilation of both the creator and creations: *khaalik khalak, khalak mein khaalik sab ghat rahyo samayi*. Putting it more simply, Kabir typically announced, as many Sufis and *sant*s would have liked to do: *kahen kabir ek ram japhu re, hindu turak na koyi!*

Indeed, free from prejudices, Kabir's language of devotion was considered a blessing for all. An early appreciation of Kabir's life and teaching may be seen in Nabhadas' famous *Bhaktamal* (*Garland of Devotees*) (*c.*1600):

> *Hindu-turak praman ramaini sabadi saakhi* |
> *Pachhpat nahin bachan sab hi ke hit ki bhashi* | |

Around the same time, *c.*1600, Anantadas composed his enchanting versified biographical text, *Parchais*, on the lives and works of the most popular *bhakti* poets of northern India in fifteenth and sixteenth centuries. Anantadas has shown how Ravidas and Dadu Dayal tried to convince Kabir of the need to transcend the *sagun/nirgun* divide as well.

Ravidas pointed out that one should not have dogmatic views about them:

> You should realize that *nirgun* and *sagun* are the same.
> You must think of *sagun* as of butter
> And *nirgun* as of heated ghee.

The appropriation of Kabir was sought to be legitimized through God miraculously appearing during the course of the conversation and entering Kabir's heart. The idea was to do away with Brahmin/Shudra distinction. Kabir would go to any length to make that happen. Did the *sant*s succeed in their mission? It is certainly time to learn from them, for it is never too late.

17

AKBAR'S CONQUEST OF THE FLOURISHING COUNTRY OF KASHMIR

SOME INSIGHTS FROM history can help in understanding the current political blitzkrieg in Kashmir. His Majesty's Voice, Abu'l Fazl's account of late sixteenth-century conquest of Kashmir under Mughal emperor Akbar gives a veritable sense of *déjà vu*, no matter from which perspective one looks at the onslaught for subjugating Kashmir by a relentlessly centralizing Indian juggernaut. The title of the celebratory chapter of the imperial ideologue's *Akbarnama*, read together with detailed annexures in the *A'in-i-Akbari*, announces violent setting up of a major milestone in the fast expanding Mughal power: 'The conquest of the flourishing country of Kashmir through the fortune of the Shahinshah'.

After briefly recounting the history of political violence in Kashmir for close to a century, especially since Akbar's father Humayun and grandfather Babur broke on the Indian political scene and their unsuccessful attempts to properly integrate Kashmir in the emerging Mughal empire, which led to frequent massacres and loss of human resources, for which there is no lamentation, Abu'l Fazl writes:

> It is an old rule that when good intention and choice action meet together in a seeker after fortune, almighty

> God grants him the easy realization of every wish that he may entertain, and even spiritual and physical successes for which he has framed no wish rise up and serve those favourites of fortune who possess those two attributes (good intention and choice action). Accordingly, the circumstances of the world's lord tell of this, and this book in some measure recites the fact of the conquest of this country as a new instance.

Thus, Akbar was able to accomplish what his father and grandfather could not.

Understandably, Abu'l Fazl, who was treated by Akbar as the closest friend and advisor, does not provide details of horrendous violence and yet mentions different ways in which the 'wicked' and 'foolish' opposition had to be neutralized, either through winning over 'untrustworthy' local collaborators or deploying massive military resources to crush any resistance. According to him,

> the soldiers prevailed over every house, and in every corner there were hot encounters (with Mughal forces taking over the rooftop of virtually every house, *sar-i khane*, to ensure complete acceptance of the fait accompli).

This was achieved through systematic planning for months, followed by massive march and deployment of large contingent of the army through all the roads to Kashmir. Abu'l Fazl relates:

> Whoever knows a little about the ravines of the road to it will understand that no thought of strange conquest troubled the minds of the inhabitants. On all four sides, mountains which raise their heads to heaven

> act as sentinels. Though there are six or seven roads, yet a large army cannot march rapidly by them, as they can also be easily blocked.

Once the entire countryside, major towns and historic seat of power, the 'divinely' created holy-city of Srinagar, were taken over, amidst reports of attacks from those still resisting and their swift and merciless shooting down, the Mughals needed legitimacy for their conquest and rule. Writing after the conquest was secured, Abu'l Fazl notes: 'At the present day that a great part of the army in Kashmir has been withdrawn, 4,892 cavalry and 92,400 infantry remain deployed'. This is a considerable number; yet it could not have sustained the conquest if it were not projected as a legitimate continuation of Kashmir's fabled four millennia of political achievements, with some aberrations in between. Thus, recourse was made to invoke the region's vibrant historical traditions, resources of powerful pundits with their own traditions going back to mythical ancient past, and legitimacy sought from Muslim holy-men, one of whom, a Sufi like figure, was approached by Abu'l Fazl himself; the name of much-respected fifteenth-century Sultan, Zainul Abidin, was also thrown in. Among the major work of larger political significance for communal harmony in society which the much venerated Sultan Zainul Abidin did was to ban cow-slaughter – a commendable move for Abu'l Fazl.

Further, the author informs:

> When the Imperial standards were for the first time borne aloft in this garden of perpetual spring, a book called *Rajatarangini* written in Sanskrit language and containing an account of the princes of Kashmir

> during a period of some four thousand years, was presented to His Majesty. It had been the custom in that country for its rulers to employ certain learned men in writing its annals. His Majesty who was desirous of extending the bounds of knowledge appointed capable interpreters in its translation which in a short time was happily accomplished.

Abu'l Fazl goes on to appropriate this history for Mughal imperial project as a continuation of Kashmir's glorious past. Thus, according to him, a long series of 191 kings had ruled throughout a period of 4,109 years, 11 months and nine days, when Akbar took over the reigns of power.

All these were listed and described with frequently provided details of enchantment with the 'heavenly' crafted geography of Kashmir (mountains, rivers, lakes, gardens, fruits and flowers symmetrically presenting it as an attractive paradise on earth). This was contrasted with repeated condemnation of its people, mainly Muslims – irrespective of whether they belonged to the sects of Sunnis, Shias or Nur Bakhshis, who originated in Iraq and deviated from both Sunni and Shia beliefs, later styling themselves as Sufis. The sectarian relations were further complicated in Kashmir with the emergence of the politically resourceful tribe of the Chaks, who were undergoing a process of religious change backed with usurpation of political power in late fifteenth and major part of the sixteenth century.

Abu'l Fazl criticizes all the active groups as people who were 'perpetually at strife with each other', especially targeting the majority Sunni and branding them as 'narrow-minded conservatives of a blind tradition'. So, for Mughal conquerors, as Abu'l Fazl states, 'the bane of this country is its people', yet they were surprised that despite a large population, 'thieving and begging are rare'. Notwithstanding, the Mughal rhetoric of backwardness or the 'scantiness of the means of subsistence' in Kashmir, they had found the country rich and flourishing, with Abu'l Fazl himself marvelling at people living in four or more storied houses, with lavish lifestyle and animalistic consumption indicating considerable prosperity. Statistical data provided by Abu'l Fazl and the general perception recorded by him indicate Kashmir was, indeed, a flourishing country that needed to be conquered.

All these were now politically secured, minus its condemned people, mainly Muslims; 'the respectable class of pundits', however, will be part of the new scheme of things. Clearly, the politically resourceful pundits and their high classical language, Sanskrit, is privileged. On the other hand, Kashmiri is depoliticized and vernacularized. As pointed out by Jadunath Sarkar, early twentieth century's foremost Indian nationalist historian, Kashmiri is an old vernacular language with a distinct dialect in Kishtwar, with further differences when used by Muslims and Hindus. Sarkar writes: 'Not only is the vocabulary of the former (Muslims) more filled with words borrowed from Persian, but also there are slight differences of pronunciation'. And, it is not the name used by the people of Kashmir itself. There the country is called Kashiru, and the language Koshiru.

According to Sarkar, called Kashmiri in Persian and Hindi, and derived from Sanskrit Kashmirika, 'Kashmiri belongs to the Dard group of the Dardic languages, and is closely related to Shina' – Indo-Aryan language of tribes of people, especially Shina or Shin, residing in the mountainous region of eastern Afghanistan, northern Pakistan, Kashmir and parts of Ladakh. Sarkar further explains, citing Grierson's *Linguistic Survey of India*:

> Since it has been for many centuries under Indian influence, and its vocabulary includes a large number of words from India, its speakers maintain that it is of Sanskritic origin, but a close examination reveals the fact that, illustrious as was the literary history of Kashmir, and learned as have been its Sanskrit pundits, this claim of Sanskrit origin cannot be sustained for the vernacular of the latter.

Not surprisingly, an otherwise verbose Abu'l Fazl was brief: 'Although Kashmir has a dialect of its own, their learned books are in the Sanskrit language'.

Thus, the loquacious vernacular mass was maimed into complete submission. Mercifully, the conquerors announced, the famously skilled Muslim 'artisans of various kinds can be deservedly employed in the greatest cities'. Conforming to the ruthless nature of the conquest, one of the first measures was to ensure the control of the revenue department directly from the centre with orders for collected revenue to be sent to imperial treasury. Abu'l Fazl typically concludes: 'Although one-third had been for a long time the nominal share of the state, more than two shares were actually taken, but through His Majesty's justice, it has been reduced to one half'. Look at the characteristic chicanery: one-third has been reduced to half!

The logic of aggressive political aggrandizement for enjoying absolute power can be absolutely ludicrous. For Abu'l Fazl, the violent subjugation and smothering of a people is a divinely sanctioned historic moment, made possible through 'good intention and choice action'. For him, any opposition, especially if it is violent, is an unacceptable and fraughtful affair, *qissa-i pur-ghussa*, as he liked to call it for the Afghan resistance to the setting up of the Mughal empire.

The Mughals reduced Kashmir to the status of a large district, pompously called *sarkar*, and attached it with the *suba* (province) of Kabul; the city of Kabul was its capital, though Ghazna was previously the seat of power. The Mughal *suba* of Kabul comprised Pakli, Bimbar, Swat, Bajaur, Qandahar, Zabulistan and Kashmir. Will the modern Moguls now aim for the larger geopolitical expansion and how? Among other things, it will involve humongous violence and large-scale destruction of human resources at the cost of which mammoth empires have always been built. As this writer likes to put it, conquerors eventually come down from their horses to govern with equanimity, doing justice to all, which provides legitimacy to their rule, else mindless political aggrandizement can only lead to further violence and resultant disintegration.

After aggressively conquering Rajasthan, Kashmir, Gujarat and Bengal, besides subjugating large swathes of territory across the Indian subcontinent, and subduing and shutting up almost all the contemporary claimants to political power, Akbar called for peace. He termed it: *sulh-i kul* (absolute peace).

NOTE

Chitralekha Zutshi has produced an excellent piece of work (2014), rising above the usual communal divide on the history of a region known for its shared cultural traditions and contested political claims.

In the language of Kalhana, Kashmir's foremost medieval historian, Zutshi's book offers *shantrasa*, calm reflection and realization, in times of political abuses, cacophony and violence.

REFERENCES

A'in-i-Akbari of Abu'l Fazl, English tr. H.S. Jarrett, second edition, edited and annotated by Sir Jadunath Sarkar, vols. II-III, reprint, Delhi: Low Price Publications, 1997.

Akbarnama of Abu'l Fazl, English tr. H. Beveridge, vol. III, reprint, Delhi: Low Price Publications, 2007.

Zutshi, Chitralekha, *Kashmir's Contested Pasts: Narratives, Sacred Geographies, and the Historical Imagination*, New Delhi: Oxford University Press, 2014.

[Earlier versions of this article have appeared in *National Herald*, 1 September 2019, and in the *Sunday Guardian*: https://www.sundayguardianlive.com/opinion/emperor-akbar-conquered-kashmir.]

18

HISTORY AND THE PRESENT: RELEVANCE OF AKBAR IN OUR TROUBLED TIMES

MANIMUGDHA SHARMA's book is a passionate plea for understanding the value of what he calls the magnificent rule of Mughal emperor, Akbar the Great (1556-1605). Working as a journalist with the *Times of India* in Delhi, the author offers, through his back and forth narrative, insights from Akbar's reign relevant to the present.

Having conquered large parts of the subcontinent through aggressive political violence and amazing tactical alliances, Akbar was able to neutralize all possible opposition for the major part of his reign. He also subdued religious groups and leaders in such a way that they were brought within the ambit of the governing principles of the state. Yet, he practised an inclusive political culture which ensured unity in diversity of the kind cherished for long in India's national imagination.

The Mughal emperors' sense of the responsibilities of the state and norms of governance are particularly important for understanding how they maintained political stability in the vast empire they founded, with a fledgling start in 1526 and brutal termination in 1857. For much of it, they ruled with equanimity, facilitating a flourishing economy and ensuring mutually respectful coexistence of a vast variety of people in large parts of the country. Military victories and open-mindedness in terms of conquest and governance were together shaped by the view that the rulers needed to dismount from their horses to govern equitably – establishing a just regime in which people were not discriminated against on religious grounds.

Customary practices apart, people were considered equal in the eyes of God, whom the rulers claimed to represent, styling themselves with titles such as Zillullah (shadow of God) and invoking the most popular Islamic formula of Allahu Akbar (God is Great). Thus, even someone like Akbar was not steering clear of religion altogether. He was, indeed, conflating religious and political categories, even if we ignore the fanciful talk of a new religion, Din-i Ilahi – imaginatively dismissed by some historians as a palace cult not followed by even the most resourceful courtiers.

Contemporary early modern European emperors were showing light on how to move forward. Since rulers had enough power and resources to build vast empires, they also considered themselves capable of controlling and governing the lives of the people. Religious justification and legitimacy was not required for political actions (see Michel Foucault's Lecture on Governmentality). The state acted in its own interest and strove for well-being of subjugated people. This also meant that the state had the capacity to kill, but it would not let anyone die. Also, just as they did not need to guilotine people for not following a particular official religion, they would also not allow violent mobs brutalizing each other on the streets and bazaars.

Contrary to what Sharma suggests, for a multi-religious country like India, a complete separation of church and state, was not possible. Rulers like Akbar recognized the multiplicity of religious traditions and practices, which were often at odds with each other, but they were not allowed to dictate terms to political regimes. The latter did intervene in issues relating to religious beliefs and sentiments, but maintained critical equidistance from all of them (for more on this theme, consult Akeel Bilgrami). This is what went on to be a typically Indian version of secularism, which is, in other words, tolerance for a melange of religious practices and communities coexisting with each other. This was ensured by the much celebrated idea of *sulh-i kul*, which can be glossed as an ethical position that encouraged respect for difference in a context in which the political regime was confident of its own finality as a divinely ordained just rule.

As Sharma has rightly pointed out, the older nationalist celebration of Akbar's greatness is now being abandoned in favour of an aggressive vilification in right-wing Hindutva propaganda; demonization of the kind that was previously restricted to someone like Aurangzeb (1658-1707). This is disappointing as formidable rulers like Akbar and Ashoka have for long been part of Indian national narrative of its glorious past – large-scale empire-building informed by social and political theories of their own (vide Rajeev Bhargava). In cultural arena, this was illustrated through Sufis, mystics and *gurus* such as Khwaja Mu'in-ud-Din Chishti, Sant Kabir and Guru Nanak. These iconic figures, too, are now being discarded by people with no idea of the world around them, forget about any worthwhile understanding of the past. In modern times, the historic role of preaching peace for respectful coexistence of a large diversity of people was picked up in a big way by Mahatma Gandhi, who paid with his life for the cause he upheld – non-violence even under extreme provocation.

In our post-truth political and cultural context, publication of books which seek to seriously engage with the past as an intellectual exercise relevant to current politics is commendable. This is especially true as the secular, liberal and cosmopolitan credentials of the country's ruling classes are taking a back seat or being abandoned altogether. Following Arjun Appadurai, parts of it can be identified as the revolt of the new autocratic elites – frustrated and angry over their suppressed aspirations which, they believe, can be corrected by whatever means. Thus, all things cherished in the past are being systematically destroyed. Will this lead to a new and better dawn through a process of constructive destruction? Or, the 'disaster capitalism' is herding us into an extended period of darkness without any guarantee of light or even life at the end of the tunnel? Certainly, there is urgent need to steer clear of the current wave of communalization of religious practices and nationalization of superstitious beliefs. Therefore, it is time to return to the history of political theory and governance for insights on how to wriggle out of the dead-end.

The professional historians, who are engaged in the production of knowledge as part of their disciplinary practice and for scholarly conversations within academic fraternities, do not generally write books for larger readership. Maintaining critical historical distance, they are expected to intervene in charged political debates in which abuse of the past is rampant. Most non-partisan historians do not succeed in this role. Most are unable to control their biases and prejudices either. For all we know, historians' commitment to any particular ideology of their time, for whatever their worth, is incompatible with objective history.

This, in turn, means that some issues are not critically thrashed for understanding what happened in the past and its contested legacy of crucial import in the present. As a mature society, we are required to come to terms with all the complexities of our past even if it sometimes involved violence, destruction and injustices – asking all questions and taking cognizance of all kinds of narratives and political positions, both in the past and the present.

As it happens, authors of popular books enjoy wide readership, but they are not fully invested in rigorous historical research. They lack access to institutional wherewithal to deploy required apparatus and follow protocols of writing history of the kind expected from professional historians. Their writings are triggered by their passion and commitment for a better informed society. Writing from a strong secular position, Sharma offers a forceful reiteration of the urgent need to learn from the past to preserve the pluralistic character of India's political culture and society. Those in the business of politics and government should definitely learn some lessons from the past for their own benefit, lessons of the kind derived from the extraordinary reign of Akbar.

The great man ruled for fifty years. His more controversial great-grandson, Aurangzeb, ruled for another fifty. His son and grandson, naturalist Jahangir (1605-27) and stylish Shah Jahan (1627-58) together presided over another fifty years or more in the first half of the seventeenth century. The empire itself took another 150 years (1707-1857) to decline and fall. Some bits of this historical experience and heritage are still relevant and can show the way to people in power on how to govern a vast country with so much diversity, without needing to massacre people to elicit complete submission. We need political stability, social security and economic well-being for all, whatever their creed. For God is supposed to have made them all and God knows best!

[Review of *Allahu Akbar: Understanding the Great Mughal in Today's India*, by Manimugdha Sharma, New Delhi: Bloomsbury, 2019. A shorter version has appeared in the *Telegraph* (Calcutta): https://m.telegraphindia.com/culture/books/book-review-allahu-akbar-understanding-the-great-mughal-in-todays-india-by-manimugdha-sharma/cid/1767493?ref=books_culture-books-page.]

19

RELIGION AND POLITICAL CULTURE IN MUGHAL INDIA

WITH NEARLY FIFTY years of research and teaching experience in the best of the universities in India and the United States, what the distinguished scholar, Professor Muzaffar Alam, has offered has the quality of a swan-song – the culmination of a lifelong intellectual activity to produce a book on a theme that was long waiting to be written and one that only he could have done on a majestic scale of this kind. With a style marked by reticence, evasion and hedging, much needed to survive in the dirty waters of medieval Indian history, Alam has taught for many years in the prestigious Jawaharlal Nehru University in New Delhi before moving two decades ago to serve as the George V. Bobrinskoy Professor in South Asian Languages and Civilizations at the University of Chicago. Besides lasting collaborative research of much value, the veteran scholar's own previous books have broken new ground. Beginning with an important intervention in the form of *The Crisis of Empire in Mughal North India, 1707-48* (1986), the author went on to write his equally famous book, *The Languages of Political Islam in India, c.1200-1800* (2004). He has now come up with this gorgeous and substantial piece of work, *The Mughals and the Sufis: Islam and Political Imagination in India, 1500-1750.*

Moving away from what he calls the traditional paradigm that champions political and fiscal history over other equally important dimensions, Alam explores in the present book the significance of critical relationships between the powerful Mughal court culture and various strands of Islamic mysticism by deploying a wide range of source material, mainly in Persian, but also in Urdu and Arabic. Some of the key texts used to write the book are still unpublished, but the author has the enviable ability and expertise to read manuscripts – gained from his early education in the famous Islamic seminary at Deoband in western Uttar Pradesh, which is often in news for its regressive stand on social and cultural issues affecting Muslim communities. The author himself takes a secular position on matters political much as he seems to be keeping critical distance from the dominant secular historiography. The central concerns of the book and broad conclusions remain within the ambit of the general consensus in academic history, dominated by the secularists, on what the Mughal political idioms were like. Yet the details the author has offered are simply awe-inspiring. As the saying goes, the devil lies in the details!

In keeping with his approach of avoiding any headlong conflict with the entrenched orthodoxies in related fields of Mughal history and yet attempting to offer something different, especially on religion and political culture which are generally studied with the felt need to emphasize on religious tolerance and communal harmony, Alam's detailed introductory discussion (listed as chapter one) does away with any systematic historiographical analysis of existing scholarship.

In the process, the usual meaningful exercise of stock-taking of the field that would set the agenda for the author has been abandoned. Instead, the Introduction offers what has been termed as a long view of Sufism and political culture in India, within Muslim intellectual traditions, from the time of the later Mughals down to the nineteenth and twentieth centuries. The key figures include Shah Waliullah (d.1762) and Saiyid Ahmad Shahid (d.1831) at one end of the spectrum and Shibli Nu'mani (d.1914) and Muhammad Iqbal (d.1938) at the other. In Alam's considered opinion, studying these later stalwarts' understanding of Islam and political imagination in the heyday of Mughal power can offer a better and informed long-term perspective than anachronistic readings of texts and historical situations, which are often the case in politically charged histories of the public domain. Academic histories are not free from these blemishes either.

Alam has thus sought to steer clear of some of the hotly debated issues such as questions of conversion and Islamization, grievances relating to cases of demolition of temples, cow-slaughter and frequent rhetoric on collection of the discriminatory tax called *jizya*, etc. Instead, a focused reading of some interesting sets of sources have been offered to show a complex picture of complicated relationships between the rulers and Sufis – important for far-reaching consequences to Mughal politics and society. This is specially so when the author takes the reader deep in the seventeenth-century underbelly of the Mughal empire, with a fascinating set of material known to experts but never properly utilized. Starting with the shaky foundations in the early-sixteenth century, under Zahiruddin Muhammad Babur and Nasiruddin Muhammad Humayun who were no less formidable figures in their own distinct styles, the Mughal empire was firmly established by the end of the century by emperor Jalaluddin Muhammad Akbar (chapter two).

With a long history of large-scale empire building in India, the Mughals were quick to grasp the norms of governance and indeed political theory required to manage and control the vast subcontinental diversity. Given the fact that religion and politics get entangled in India with terrible consequences even in the twenty-first century, religious justification of political power in Indian history has been a fait accompli for long. Men of religion needed political patronage and protection, and rulers needed legitimacy from the former on account of their popular appeal. The intercession by holy men also meant divine blessings procured directly from God and His Prophets and other representatives on earth, in this case important figures and shrines of the popular saints such as Khwaja Gharib Nawaz Mu'in-ud-Din Chishti of Ajmer.

Living legends from a variety of Sufi lineages such as the Chishti, Suhrawardi, Firdausi, Shattari and Qadiri were active in India with a long history behind them. They were known for being committed to what is professed as the Shariat or Muslim law, and yet free from the bigotry or fanaticism that is generally associated with custodians of Islam, the theologians (*ulama*). They were also free from communal biases in relation to non-Muslims, identifiable as Hindus and sectarianism of the kind that sought to vilify communities of Muslims such as the Shias. The value of this approach was quickly realized by the Mughals, who needed to maintain a critical distance from the Central Asian strand of Sufism which came in the wake of the conquest, the Naqshbandis, who combined their mysticism with aggressive accumulation of wealth and assertion of uncompromising commitment to Sunni Hanafi interpretation of Islamic principles.

The struggle between the two strands of Sufism – accommodation and compromises in the given situation of the Indian environment and extraordinary emphasis on Islamic piety bordering on Sunni fanaticism on the other – marks the defining feature of Mughal-Sufi relations from the late sixteenth century onward. The inclusive Mughal imperial culture privileged Indian Rajputs and Iranian Shias, identified itself as part of a broad and liberal Islamic political and cultural tradition, and understood the value of devotional practices of the kind the Chishtis and the Qadiris upheld. This latter position was powerfully articulated by the seventeenth-century Sufi scholar belonging to the Chishti-Sabiri order and hailing from Awadh, Shaikh Abdur Rahman Chishti (d. 1683), in his voluminous writings. One set of his compositions, *Mir'atul Asrar*, which is a huge collection of Sufi biographies prefaced with a detailed exposition of some of the important features of Sufism, has been used by Alam, in chapter three, to show how it was possible to remain within the fold of Islam and yet be eclectic in the manner in which Indian Sufism has been. Sufis do not need to be bound to any narrow interpretation of Islam and in doing so they can be free from the usual biases of the kind Sunni theologians and Naqshbandi Sufis betrayed.

The author has pitted the more acceptable Chishti position in Mughal India quoting Abdur Rahman as writing that Sufis have no *mazhab*, or commitment to any juridical school of Sunni Islam, against a rhetorical statement of the leading Naqshbandi Sufi Shaikh Ahmad Sirhindi (d. 1624), who is also styled and venerated in some strands of Islamic traditions as Mujaddid Alf-i Sani, or renovator of Islam in the second millennium of the Hijri calendar. Sirhindi had remarked that if a prophet were sent among Muslims of his time, he would have practised the Hanafi interpretation of Islam. There were few takers for this kind of assertion in the Mughal system and yet the sons and grandsons of Sirhindi were able to make considerable inroads to the extent that they were much privileged by the time Aurangzeb takes over in the middle of the seventeenth century. It served both – Aurangzeb needed legitimacy for his horrible butchery inside the imperial household and the Naqshbandis coveted power and prestige which the early ancestors of their spiritual lineage enjoyed in Central Asia. This is to the extent that the son and leading successor of Sirhindi in his Naqshbandi-Mujaddidi order, Shaikh Muhammad Ma'sum (d. 1669), sought to own responsibility for the execution of the saintly prince and Shah Jahan's heir apparent, Dara Shukoh (d. 1656) with his own hands, with reference to a dream in which he received a sword from God to do away with the latter. The horrendous bloodshed and transformation of Mughal polity under Aurangzeb, with the Naqshbandis getting entrenched in the Mughal court and outside, is narrated by Alam in the last chapter.

This was at the cost of a huge investment in what is identified as cultural synthesis relevant to sustain the empire. The result was a complete mayhem by the end of Aurangzeb's reign. His immediate successors, who were nominated and backed by the Naqshbandi-Mujaddidi Sufis, made a mess of it. The more eclectic approach of the kind Sufis of the Chishti and Qadiri orders were proposing and important figures like Dara Shukoh and his equally accomplished sister, Jahanara (d. 1681), were adopting as social and political ideologies relevant for the time, have been brought in interesting detail by the author. Besides the hagiography and defence of Indian Sufism by Abdur Rahman Chishti in his *Mira'tul Asrar*, the Sufi writer composed a few other powerful treatises aimed at transcending differences between religious beliefs and communities. One of the texts, *Mira't-i Madariya* (studied in chapter four), appropriated the fifteenth-century popular mystic figure, Shah Badi-ud-Din Madar, whose extraordinary career began as a prodigious Jewish child in Syria and whose shrine (*dargah*), is located in Kanpur, Uttar Pradesh. Tradition claimed that he was directly guided by God, the prophets (Moses, Jesus and Muhammad), celestial beings and the leading saint of India, Mu'in-ud-Din Chishti of Ajmer. Thus, he was very much identified as part of the Chishti tradition, even though many of his practices appeared heretical, or outside the pale of Islam, with his close disciples styling themselves as *yogis* or *dashnami sannyasis*, sunk in artificially created ecstasy with the help of intoxicants such as *hashish* and *ganja* and puffing with chants of Dam Madar.

Abdur Rahman also composed a brilliantly imagined text, called *Mira'tul Makhluqaat* (analysed in chapter five), claiming it to be a translation of an ancient Indian Sanskrit textual genre known in Mughal intellectual circles as the Puranas. The translations of *Ramayana* and *Mahabharata* were already known since the time of Akbar. Abdur Rahman had himself translated the *Bhagavad-Gita* into Persian. These were done with the dual process of their interpretations, oral or written, in Awadhi and Braj versions of medieval Hindi, before putting them into writing in Persian. *Mira'tul*

Makhluqaat is extraordinary in the sense that it showcased how the Brahmanical Hindu mythical time of ancient gods were very much part of the Islamic notion of time since the arrival of Adam on earth. Ancient gods belonged to the people of *jinn*s, made of fire, and descendants of Adam, including Hindus, are human beings, made of soil. The *jinn*s were ordered to withdraw to mountains, giving space to humans, but they could also be deployed to take care of injustices in the world, as in the case of the battle of Mahabharata. This being a Kaliyuga, it can also witness the horrendous violence on the family of the Prophet, especially the martyrdom of his grandson, Husain, by miscreants identified as bastards (*haramzada*s), apostates (*murtadd*) and barbarians (*malechh*). These condemnations are attributed by Abdur Rahman Chishti to Mahadeva (Shiva), who in turn is supposedly narrating these episodes to his wife Parvati, who is shown as being keen to know about Adam and Prophet Muhammad (Mahamat).

Alam's details from this work are blended equally interestingly in the next chapter (six), in which Dara Shukoh works with a battery of pundits on a new translation in Persian of *Yogavasistha*. Whereas till the time of Akbar, the Hindu traditions were beginning to be known through translations in line with the policy of *sulh-i kul*, peace with all, by Dara Shukoh's time in the middle of the seventeenth century it was possible to imagine that the powerful Mughal prince could style himself after the ideal Hindu king, Lord Rama of Ayodhya. This was the aim behind Dara's preparation of *Yogavasistha*, mentioned in the beginning of the text itself about the prince seeing a dream in which he was seeking blessings from the Sage Vasistha, in front of Rama who is placed on a higher pedestal and styled as an elder brother. On Vasistha's advice Rama embraced him with great love, and also passed on the sweetmeat given by the former. This was taken as the sign for getting a new translation of the text done, which was in line with translations and studies of other texts seeking common ground for Islam and Hindu traditions, symbolically referred to as the merging of the two oceans, in a text with the title *Majma-ul-Bahrain*. None of these were found to be contradictory to Dara Shukoh's commitment for Sufism and Sufi figures from the past, and attachment to Qadiri Sufi saints of his own time. That there was no difference between Hindus and Muslims was also supported by the doctrine of *wahdatul wujud*, unity of being, which was similar to Advaita Vedanta. But the no holds barred emphasis on these ideas for a common and harmonious public culture was used by Aurangzeb as a pretext to remove Dara in his bid to capture the Mughal throne.

This violent move created a huge difficulty within the Mughal household as well. Alam has discussed this in his penultimate and detailed 72-page chapter (seven), pointing to the contested loyalties of Mughal princesses, but focusing on their remarkable devotional and intellectual investments. This is especially with reference to three of them – Shah Jahan's daughters Jahanara and Raushanara (d.1671), and Aurangzeb's daughter Zebun Nisa (d.1701). Jahanara was close to her father and Dara Shukoh and, following the latter, heavily devoted to Sufism, with deep attachment with Mu'in-ud-Din Chishti and his shrine, and also becoming a disciple of the leading Qadiri Sufi in Kashmir, Mulla Shah Badakhshi (d.1661), with a couple of books on Sufism to her own credit. In the terrible war of succession, she had sided with Dara Shukoh and tried to reason with Aurangzeb for sanity without success. Mercifully for her, Aurangzeb did not create any difficulties for her subsequently, but he did not follow her will to be fully implemented. As the richest Mughal princess of the time, she had left behind a sum of three crore rupees to be distributed among the attendants of the Chishti shrines, but Aurangzeb allowed only a third of it to be distributed as per some reading of the Shariat that he adhered to.

Jahanara's younger and less accomplished sister, Raushanara had sided with Aurangzeb in the struggle for power. She was pampered by him with some independence and creature comforts with a mansion outside the fort. Her love life was a matter of gossip in public, which also questioned her untimely demise at the age of 53, with doubting Thomases suspecting that Aurangzeb ordered her to be poisoned to death. Alam has given details of her long correspondence with the young Naqshbandi-Mujaddidi Sufi, Shaikh Saifuddin, operating from the Mughal court with access to ladies of the harem. The letters, the ones written by the Sufi have survived, refer to the princess cultivating mystical whispers of the heart, *zikr-i dil.* Saifuddin was convinced Raushanara had reached the stage where she could be recognized as an accomplished Sufi in her own right. From there she could have only grown as a Sufi teacher, poet and writer, but that was not to be – whatever the truth relating to her death.

Aurangzeb doted on his genius daughter, Zebun Nisa, exposing her to the best of the teachers of the time, but as it happens, involvement in politics proved to be her nemesis. She had the guts to support a brother who had rebelled against their father for whom ruthless power was beyond all bonds. She was promptly put under arrest, with some freedom to continue her scholarly pursuits, mainly reading works of poetry and composing some of her own, published under an apt pen-name, Makhfi (hidden one). Among the people she was allowed to correspond with was Shaikh Abdul Ahad Wahdat (d.1713), as is understandable a Naqshbandi old man – grandson of Shaikh Ahmad Sirhindi. Wahdat is known in posterity as a fine poet who wrote with the pen-name, Gul (rose). One of his letters to Zebun Nisa, includes this fine couplet in Persian:

> *Bas kunam gar in sukhan afzun shawad |*
> *Khwud jigar chi bud ke khara khun shawad | |*
>
> (I should stop, for if I speak further
> Not just the liver, even a stone will bleed).

According to reports, mentioned by Alam, Aurangzeb cried on hearing the news of Zebun Nisa's death and ordered a tomb to be built over her grave. Though privileging the puritanical Naqshbandis all his life, Aurangzeb himself was subsequently buried at the Chishti centre of Khuldabad in the Deccan (1707). By then, the Mughal state was in a terrible crisis, but its foundations were deeply embedded in the country's composite culture. It took a long 150 years to decline and fall with a final and vengeful push from the British in 1857. The last Mughal emperor, Bahadur Shah Zafar, died reciting some painful Sufi poetry in faraway Rangoon. The author and publisher deserve commendations for bringing out this magnificent piece of work.

[Review of Muzaffar Alam, *The Mughals and the Sufis: Islam and Political Imagination in India, 1500-1750*, Ranikhet:

Permanent Black, in association with Ashoka University, 2021, pp. xiii + 454. Price: Rs. 1095. Published in the *Frontline*, 11 February 2022. URL: https://frontline.thehindu.com/books/book-review-the-mughals-and-the-sufis-by-muzaffar-alam-explores-the-sufi-influence-in-mughal-rule/article38308607.ece.]

20

NUR JAHAN AND THE FASCINATING WORLD OF MUGHAL WOMEN

HISTORIANS ARE increasingly coming out from the ivory towers of academia and its elitist intellectual discourse to engage with larger readership of the popular domain. In doing so, they are able to deploy current historical research for informing and educating non-historians and general readers on themes of topical interest or offering interesting biographies of charismatic figures of the past. Ruby Lal's book, *Empress: The Astonishing Reign of Nur Jahan*, is one such attempt of critical importance.

Mughal women are known for their powerful presence, both when they lived in army camps during political flux and when they were sequestered in segregated harems during political stability. In the early period of the making of the Mughal empire, the kings would reveal their temptations for good looking young boys; once the powerful empire was established, the emperors styled themselves as big Indian patriarchs.

Lal herself has set the agenda straight:

> My work as a feminist historian has focused on two interrelated questions: First, how can I best tell the

> stories of women and girls, which are largely missing from the pre-colonial and colonial history of South Asia? Then, what counts as evidence, and therefore as history? One answer to both questions has involved using sources that other historians have ignored.

Lal has also employed her feminist gaze to see what men writing in the seventeenth and eighteenth centuries had to say about a remarkable seventeenth-century woman, Nur Jahan, who has been portrayed by the author as something of a proto-feminist and an Empress in her own right.

Some very interesting work on women and questions relating to gender in medieval and early modern India has emerged in recent decades, but no amount of writing is enough on the resourceful Mughal women who turned Mughal politics and rule inside out. This is particularly significant because women asserted themselves at a time when they were being invisibilized in well-guarded harem from the time of the most powerful emperor Akbar (1556-1605).

As Lal has mentioned, growing up in Fatehpur-Sikri and Agra, and probably living there until her marriage, Nur Jahan's parents would have ensured that their daughters would be known for intelligence, piety, self-control, good judgement, tenderness, and temperate speech. Texts in circulation on norms of comportment would also recommend that girls should be brought up to keep close to the house and live in seclusion and develop qualities required to make good wives, for which they did not need to be taught to read and write.

However, Mughal women were often highly accomplished scholars, writers, poets and intellectuals, either through their personal excellence and initiatives to break free from any restrictions or because of the fact that Mughal India was not such a regressive place to inhabit. 'The comfortable coexistence of Hindu *raja*s and the Mughals, of Hindavi and Persian, the Bible and the Quran, the orthodox and the heterodox', in sum, 'the diversity of beliefs and practices made Akbar's India a charmed place'.

Emperor Jahangir (1605-27) built upon the broad-based Akbari dispensation, which in turn invoked the experience and expertise of Babur and Humayun (reflected among other accounts in the narrative prepared by formidable personality of Babur's daughter Gulbadan Begum). The Mughals also invoked their Chingizi and Timurid legacy and drew on historical experience of various Muslim Sultanates, established in India since the thirteenth century, which also witnessed the exceptional rise and rule of Raziya Sultan. The latter was nominated by her own father, Sultan Iltutmish who established the Delhi Sultanate on a firm footing.

Jahangir's granddaughters, Raushan Ara and Jahan Ara, are also known for their strong and divergent political stands during the war of succession, which led to Aurangzeb (1658-1707) capturing power by eliminating his brothers and incarcerating his father emperor Shah Jahan (1628-58). Jahan Ara's mother and Shah Jahan's favourite wife, Mumtaz Mahal, in whose honour the emperor built the Taj Mahal, was a daughter of Nur Jahan's brother, the powerful minister Asaf Khan. Nur Jahan and Asaf Khan were among the talented children of I'timad ud-Daula Ghiyas Beg, one of the most distinguished Iranian nobles of the Mughal empire.

Thus, Nur Jahan belonged to a highly influential family of Persian aristocratic background, with father, brother and first husband enjoying considerable power. When brought to Jahangir's harem as widow of Sher Afghan, the Iranian-Mughal administrator of Burdawan in Bengal, she was 'thirty-one years old, attractive, dignified, and well trained in the behaviour and duties required of noblewomen connected with palace society'. Meanwhile, Jahangir had already married as many as nineteen times, had a flock of concubines, and was adored by senior harem women. As Lal points out: 'Political ambition, intrigue, and aspirations cultivated in the harem were tightly entwined with courtly matters', the harem thus offered women surprising opportunities – 'wide horizons behind high walls'. Not long after her marriage with Jahangir, as his twentieth wife, Nur Jahan goes on to eliminate all opposition and competition to control and dominate the emperor's private and public life.

The family's hold on the emperor is further strengthened by Nur Jahan marrying her daughter from her first marriage, Ladli Begum with Jahangir's youngest son, Shahryar, from an unnamed concubine, besides marrying her niece Arjumand Banu (daughter of Asaf Khan) with Khurram, the future Mughal emperor Shah Jahan. As reports indicate, Nur Jahan herself assumed enough power to issue *farmans*, get coins struck in her name and shoot tigers as a mark of her hunting ability, which in turn symbolized imperial power and dominance. Together all these constituted her claims on sovereignty, which according to Lal was self evident for the major part of her association with Jahangir, as co-sovereign or a pair of sovereigns. Her later attempts to push for Shahryar as a possible successor of Jahangir created an unbridgeable rift not only between her and Khurram, who rebels and eventually takes over, but also with her brother Asaf Khan. Mercifully, they ensured that she will lead a dignified retired life in

Lahore till she passed away, nearly two decades after Jahangir's death.

Since the book is written like a historical novel, or as a possible pre-script for a drama or another movie on Nur Jahan, and not a conventional historical biography aimed at critical scrutiny, approval and recognition from experts in Mughal history, the latter should not crib about any acts of omission or commission on the part of the author. Nur Jahan is such a charismatic figure that anything written on her should be taken as an opportunity to know and discuss her extraordinary life.

In continuation of her somewhat exaggerated deference for the enigmatic charm of the remarkable personality of Nur Jahan, Lal says: 'In act after act – hunting, advising, issuing imperial orders and coins, designing buildings – she ensured that her name was etched indelibly in public memory and history'. Unfortunately for Nur Jahan and her biographer, the theologians never read *khutba* (Friday sermon) in her name, which would truly make her a legitimate empress of Hindustan. Instead, she was generally dismissed as a gold-digger, scheming and mischievous woman, whose ambitious political manoeuvres and aggressive interventions in matters of governance caused much consternation. For some opponents, it was a veritable *fitna* – a seditious enterprise of disastrous consequences.

[Review of *Empress: The Astonishing Reign of Nur Jahan*, by Ruby Lal, Rs. 599, Penguin. A shorter version has been published in the *Telegraph*: https://m.telegraphindia.com/culture/books/the-remarkable-life-of-mughal-empress-nur-jahan/cid/1683944?ref=culture_culture-page.]

21

JAFAR ZATALLI: EXPOSING FAKE PROPRIETY OF THOSE IN POWER

MIR MUHAMMAD JAFAR ZATALLI, who lived in the second half of the seventeenth and the first decade of the eighteenth century, is often dismissed or ignored by modern scholars for his alleged vulgarity. Nevertheless, he enjoys the distinction of being the first major Urdu literary figure who attempted to redraw the boundaries of what was considered permissible in literature. Belonging to a Sayyid family of Narnaul, in Haryana, Jafar Zatalli addressed issues of morality, particularly among the Mughal elite, including the princes and nobles. His writings have often been overlooked as mere *laffazi* (facile eloquence) of little value. He even represented himself as a *zatalli* (idle talker), as we can see from his *takhallus* (nom de plume). Yet, no historian of Urdu language and literature can afford to ignore Zatalli and his work.

Contrary to the indifferent attitude of the historians of medieval India towards him, it is important to note that Zatalli heralded a linguistic turn of sorts by publicly exposing the rampant duplicities of Mughal society through his satire and poetry of protest, which were in a no holds barred language – an idiom that was hitherto restricted to the oral domain. He wrote of love and sex in a way that no one had done before him in Mughal India. His oeuvre also pre-dated the poetry of love and/or self-flagellation over unfulfilled desire, *ghazal*, which subsequently emerged as the dominant form in the next generation, though satire in Urdu also grew into an important trope for resistance and protest in north India in the first half of the eighteenth century.

Zatalli, however, wrote during the period when the poets were still mixing Persian and Urdu expressions in their compositions. Their language was called *rekhta* – gibberish or mixed language. The eighteenth-century sophistication of Urdu language had not yet come about and an accomplished *ustad* like Siraj-ud-Din Ali Khan-i-Arzu (1687-1756) was yet to emerge. Khan-i-Arzu corrected and polished the language of many Urdu poets who flocked to Delhi, and some of them went on to be counted amongst the all time greats – Mir Taqi Mir, Muhammad Rafi Sauda and Khwaja Mir Dard come to mind immediately.

As mentioned earlier, Jafar Zatalli's compositions, both prose and poetry, are amongst the earliest examples of *rekhta* or early Urdu. Even as he used established Persian literary conventions, he often departed from tradition to showcase his mastery of Urdu. Therefore, in many instances, his work reads like a mixed language. Sometimes, a couplet in Persian is followed by another in Urdu. In yet another case, one line of a couplet is in Persian, and the next in Urdu. Also, Persian and Urdu expressions are sometimes used in the same line, providing a spectacular example of literary and cultural appropriation.

Though the Urdu that has come down to modern times

took its mature shape only in the early eighteenth century during the period of Mughal decline, Zatalli's Urdu prose and poetry serve as interesting early examples of literary exercises in this language, executed with considerable finesse. His juxtaposition of a large vocabulary of Indic words, phrases and proverbs with Persian expressions shows the ease and flair with which he was able to transcend the barriers of language and culture.

Jafar Zatalli compiled his compositions from across a variety of literary genres in his *Kulliyat* (collected works), *Zatal-nama*, during the latter half of Aurangzeb's reign, that is, the last quarter of the seventeenth century. It is possible that Zatalli's work was subsequently edited and updated by the poet himself or by some later poets and writers. Even if some portions of the work were possibly falsely ascribed to Zatalli, it is significant that the themes covered by the poet as well as his language and form were of interest to the Urdu-reading public. In addition, he was clearly imitated by his contemporaries and certainly by later poets, including several well-known literary figures from the first half of the eighteenth century. However, none could surpass Zatalli in crudeness and in his carefree knitting together of phrases from backgrounds as diverse as theological and virtuous Arabic, polished and deceptive Persian, and rustic and direct Hindustani. Some examples of such usage will be noted below in the samples of his compositions. See, for instance, on Kam Bakhsh screwing a goat:

Zahe shah-e wala guhar kam bakhsh |
Ke ghachchi buz kard pichchi wa pakhsh ||

(Well done! Jewel of the prince, Kam Bakhsh

The little opening of the goat is ruptured into a gaping hole.)

Zatalli also wrote an outrageous *Gandu-nama* on the reign of Aurangzeb's son and successor, Bahadur Shah:

Hukm-e qazi, muhtasib za'il shude
Dil badhakar gand marawwa kheliye
Pir se aur baap se, ustad se
Chhup-chhupakar gand marawwa kheliye

In the first couplet, the poet exposes the extent of sexual transgressions (in this case, *gand marawwa* or 'anus-sex') that occurred despite the presence of the *qazi*s (Muslim judges) and *muhtasib*s (censor officials), whose powers were in decline (*za'il shude*). In the second one, he points out how this was done, playfully, away from the gaze of (*chhup-chhupakar*) the father (*baap*), teacher (*ustad*) or the religious guide (*pir*).

By contrast, on the powerful Aurangzeb himself, he wrote a *qasida* celebrating his rule and *marsiya* on his death. In his eulogy (*Dar tarif Aurangzeb*), the poet extolled the extraordinary bravery and steadfastness of Aurangzeb, which created a flutter (*khalbali*) in the Deccan (*zahe dhak-e aurangshah-e bali/dar aqlim-e dakkhan pari khalbali*). Another couplet projected Aurangzeb as an exceptional warrior who could stand on the battlefield like an unmoveable mountain (*mahasur, joddha, bali be-badal/chu al-burz qaayam, chu parbat atal*).

On the other hand, his rivals in Deccan such as Sikandar Hasan, ruler of Bijapur, Abul Hasan Tana-Shah, ruler of Golconda and Shivaji's son, Sambhaji, among others, are belittled as insignificant creatures. Zatalli reserved his worst comments for Sambhaji's agent, Pratap, whom he addressed with the rhetorical remark, *che jhant ast partab ibn-ul-hammar*, which refers to Pratap as an ass or son of a donkey and dismisses him as male pubic hair.

In this context, Zatalli also attacked Aurangzeb's sons who, according to him, not only complicated the proper and efficient management of the Deccan campaigns, but also spoiled the whole project (*hame kar-o-baar-e pidar bhand kard*). In particular, the poet pointed to their relentless propensity towards sex and wrote that chatting and fantasizing about the wet vagina or anus were a round-the-clock obsession for them (*rahe raat din gaand ke zikr mein/be-lahu luab chut ki fikr mein*).

Understandably, the butt end of his jokes were also women. Zatalli claimed, in a composition that highlights a traditional saying, that the penis can never subdue the vagina, despite all the controlling powers of society (*suni baat mayen pir fartut se/ke lauda na jita kabhi chut se*). (Remember: Polite company calls for purity of tongue and to block out offensive speech, a normative text would recommend plugging your ears with your fingers. Gossip, lies, insults and all kinds of unbridled speech were considered abhorrent and dishonourable; so too were displays of anger, haughtiness and bravado.) Zatalli wouldn't care.

However, realizing that his literary transgressions and relentless attacks on Aurangzeb's sons meant violations of established norms of conduct, Zatalli warns himself to be careful and refrain from offending his own powerful patrons. Incidentally, Kam Bakhsh and Bahadur Shah were among those who had offered patronage to Zatalli. Witnessing the terrible struggles between the sons of Aurangzeb for the Mughal throne and revealing the anxieties caused by the political crisis, Zatalli concluded his elegy on the emperor by warning himself of the consequences of his remarks in the changed scenario: *baya, jafar, sukhan ra mukhtasar kun/ze daur-e mukhtalif dar dil hazar kun* (literally: come on, Jafar, cut short your utterances; the time has changed, keep it to your heart).

Eventually, Zatalli paid with his life for criticizing Farrukh-Siyar's penchant for killing his opponents by smothering them using a leather-belt. The poet was similarly asphyxiated by the order of the emperor, *badshah-e tasme-kush farrukh-siyar*, King Farrukh-Siyar, who kills by the leather-belt. It is possible that the ruler was affronted not so much for being condemned as a *tasme-kush*, but for the poet's mocking his unjust rule, when he had just sat on the throne (1713-19). As one early biographer of Zatalli recorded, *mizaj-e padshah barham gasht, ishan ra be-jannat farastaad* ('The emperor was outraged; he, the poet, was dispatched to heaven!').

Parts of a couplet he had himself composed gives the year of his death:

> *'Haveli' chhod, yu bola zatalli*
> *'Andheri gor mein latkan lage paag'*

Computing the numerical equivalent of the second line (*andheri gor mein latkan lage paag* or 'the legs were hanging in the dark grave') as well as leaving out the numbers derived from the word *haveli* (mansion; *haveli chhod*: a mansion which was to be vacated), the year of Zatalli's execution is poetically arrived at AH 1125 (1713).

The poet identified himself as: *lallu pattu, walad indhan jangli, mutawattin andher nagri, mulazim-e sarkar-e chaupatabad/*

a loquacious sycophant and son of a wild beast, who lived in *andher nagri* (literally, city of darkness) and worked in the service of the ruler of *chaupatabad* (a ruined or despicable habitation), which is such a powerful metaphor for the deteriorating grandeur of the city of Shahjahanabad, Delhi. Indeed, the Bindaas poets, satirists and comedians have continuously called out the moral and ethical bankruptcy of those who occupy the seat of power in Delhi. For us, Jafar Zatalli is exceptional in his expertise of making a mockery of the fake propriety of those in power.

[Reference: Zatalli's *Kulliyaat, Zatal-nama*, used here is prepared by one of the most accomplished editors of Urdu literary classics, Rashid Hasan Khan, published by Anjuman Taraqqi Urdu (Hind). Extracted from my book, *The Muslim Question: Understanding Islam and Indian History* (Penguin).]

22

POWER, MEMORY AND ARCHITECTURE: A REVIEW

THE EMOTIONALLY charged partisans of Telangana and Andhra Pradesh might like to reflect on the historical experience of the region. Two distinguished American historians – Richard Eaton and Philip Wagoner – have offered a path-breaking study of monumental scale for a fascinating new account of political and cultural heritage of medieval Deccan. Eaton is the foremost scholar of South Asian Islam at the University of Arizona, Tucson, and Wagoner a fine art historian at Wesleyan University, Middletown. In addition to its significance as a collaborative effort of contemporary topical interest, this richly illustrated magnum opus presents a rigorous analysis of some of the hotly debated themes and issues in Indian history.

The Mughal-centrism in medieval Indian history being a major limitation, the finely crafted work provides a superb corrective by focusing on India's Deccan Plateau in the relatively neglected period, 1300–1600. Indeed, despite the dominance of northern India in the study of medieval history as in the politics of the present, some of the finest works of recent decades on religious movements, visual cultures, and literary traditions pertaining to the medieval period are spatially located in southern India. The monograph by Eaton and Wagoner excels in effortlessly merging a conventional historian's archival research, an art historian's fieldwork for visual data, an archaeologist's digging into mounds for material evidence of historical value, and a geographer using latest technology to map the specificity of a location to write a history of some otherwise secondary sites (Kalyana, Raichur, and Warangal) of considerable importance in the geopolitics of sixteenth-century Deccan.

The power struggle – especially involving Bijapur, Golconda, and Vijayanagara – witnessed effective deployment of three important nodes – political and historical memory, architectural heritage, and military innovations, particularly the sophisticated new gunpowder technology. The memories and monuments of earlier political achievements of the Chalukyas, including temples, relics, and city-gates, were used by Vijayanagara rulers who clearly identified themselves with an Indic or Sanskritic inheritance, but also adopted Persianate-markers such as distinctive titles and dress. Outsmarting their more resourceful rival, the Deccani Sultans also intelligently transcended the chasm between Perso-Islamic (including Shia-Sunni divide) and the Sanskritic cosmopolis – re-using Kakatiya antiques and yet creating something of their own. The extraordinary careers of Shitab Khan of Warangal, originally a low-caste Telugu warlord Chittapa and Sultan Quli, coming from Hamadan, the predominantly Turkish-speaking western Iranian province, epitomize the dynamics of the enterprise.

Further, the question of Hindu-Muslim encounter and communal relations remains important here as well. Instead of the simplistic binary of two narrow religions locked in eternal strife, the authors pursue an alternative analytical approach to understand two cosmopolitan cultural systems – Sanskritic and Persian – going beyond religious struggles as we understand in modern times. Thus, the attitude towards places of worship varied, depending upon political contexts, from spectacular theatrics to utter indifference: aggressive desecration, re-assemblage, ritual redefinition, active patronage, or sheer apathy. The most fascinating example is found in a Sanskrit inscription (10 November 1326) of Muhammad bin Tughlaq ordering restoration and protection of a Shiva Temple at Kalyana; two separate contemporary reports have added gory details of brutal punishment given to the violent vandals in proportion to their crime – the nature and seriousness of which was determined by the so-called maverick Sultan in his own inimitable style.

Apart from memory and architecture, the significance of gunpowder and military technology have also been examined, more generally with reference to the two fateful battles of Raichur (1520) and Talikota (1565). Large-scale military modernization in the intervening period of 45 years between the two battles – developing newer and better guns and designing and building taller bastions or cavaliers – by Muslim Sultanates, especially Bijapur, was in contrast to the complacency of self-assurance, indeed sheer arrogance, of Vijayanagara rulers. Kiss my foot, a confident Krishna Rai had famously demanded from the suppressed Bijapur's Ismail Adil Khan.

Thus, invoking older imperial memories and re-using architectural remains of cultural value were important tropes in the justification of power, which, in turn, meant occupation and maintenance of forts and cities as well as controlling resources and developing new centres. The foundation of the millennial city of Hyderabad (Hijri 1000/1591-92 CE) for its multi-ethnic elite, but modelled on Warangal and amidst the Telugu-speaking population of Telangana, is a case of crucial import to the current debate on the bifurcation of Andhra Pradesh. Even though electoral compulsions have now reduced political strategies to just managing vote-banks of different kinds and manipulating numbers of seats, the warring parties should, perhaps, go back to history for some fresh insights and perspectives: *Power, Memory, Architecture: Contested Sites on India's Deccan Plateau, 1300–1600* (New Delhi: Oxford University Press, 2014).

[Previously published in the *Sunday Guardian*: http://www.sunday-guardian.com/analysis/reflect-on-deccans-history.]

23

EARLY MODERN BENGAL: AN EARTHLY PARADISE

THIS WRITE-UP is based on my Introduction to the collection of essays, *An Earthly Paradise: Trade, Politics and Culture in Early Modern Bengal*, co-edited with Dr Tilottama Mukherjee. The study of history of Bengal tends to get enmeshed in and influenced by massive transformations which happened in the nineteenth century. In the process, the fascinating history of Bengal of the early modern era (sixteenth-eighteenth centuries) is almost entirely overshadowed and neglected, whereas new research shows there is so much to know about Bengal in relation to what was happening in the Indian subcontinent and globally in this period. The essays in this volume highlight these complexities and connections.

These centuries witnessed the advent of many European merchants and travellers visiting Bengal to discover its abundance of riches – both natural resources and manufactured items of its enviable enterprise. By the end of the seventeenth century, they had come to the firm conclusion, as an English East India Company employee and writer, Alexander Hamilton, did, that Bengal was an earthly paradise of a peculiar kind. Its reputation as the wealthiest province of the vast Mughal empire and an important centre in the global trading network of the early modern era attracted many to it.

The current volume points to significant strides made in the divergent fields of Bengal's early modern scholarship in the last two decades or so. Diverse themes in politics, trade and culture are covered using a wide variety of vernacular sources, besides returning to the conventional European Company archival material for fresh substantiation and validation.

Indeed, early modern Bengal bore witness to a plurality of developments in various spheres, which requires more discussion. The first five chapters in this volume, in particular, attempt to look at the diversity of Europeans coming into the region and their experiences as travellers and representatives of European companies, and the ways in which the latter negotiated with local society to establish themselves with varying degrees of success. Tilottama Mukherjee (chapter 2) writes that a wide assortment of European travellers passed through Bengal and were motivated by various factors, especially corporate greed of European traders and companies.

Further, as Gargi Chattopadhyay has shown (chapter 3), the Portuguese presence at nodal points along the Bhagirathi, including Sagor island, as well as the overshadowing presence of the Arakanese towards the east, contributed to the political turmoil of Bengal. One particular group of pirates known as the Magh or Rakhine marauders were especially feared for their daring raids enabled by an enviable ability to cover not only large parts of the littoral but also infiltrate the interior through inter-connected rivers and water channels, using lightly-made and swiftly-moving boats.

The image of the contradictory character of a hell-like

earthly paradise recurs in the sixteenth- and seventeenth-century European accounts of Bengal (as they do in the Mughal chronicles as well). They condemned it for being ruled by the mighty and greedy Muslim rulers, with its poor and slavish subjects, cunning money-grabbing traders, hot and oppressive climate, wild and untamed terrain, and yet with riches ready for plunder.

Much attention has been paid in scholarship and political discourse to the English East India Company because of the political power it would eventually gain to establish a truly colonial regime, something which the Portuguese and other Europeans could not do in Bengal. The boards of directors of other companies, such as the Verenigde Oost-Indische Compagnie (VOC), pretended that their only motive was commercial gain with no interest in territorial aggrandisement. Examining the goals of the VOC and its officials, as well as their relations with the Mughal authorities and local business partners in Bengal, Byapti Sur has illustrated (chapter 4) how the Company officials in seventeenth-century Bengal sought to claim their moral authority through various strategies.

Working through the General Imperial India Company (GIC) records in the Antwerp City archives, Wim De Winter has illustrated in detail the cultural difficulties and a number of tantalizing violations by the Company's haughty representatives, which almost sunk its business interests. They survived for a time through local intervention before fizzling out not long after (chapter 5). The Nawab of Murshidabad, while allowing the GIC representatives to conduct their business, had observed that Europeans were not men of their word as they pretended to be. He expected them to understand the value of courtly ceremonials – whether it be elaborate greetings, *taslimat* or the offering of betel (*paan*) – before permissions and announcements regarding commercial transactions were made.

Indeed, officers working for other European Companies were more discreet in their utterances and activities, and succeeded because of their ability to adapt well to local conditions. The French East India Company and its officers, for instance, worked in a functional organizational structure. Starting in 1664, under the direct authority of the French crown, its formal organization and management structure came to be established by the time that its base in Chandernagore was laid in 1693 through a *farman* issued by the Bengal Nawab. Sandip Munshi's detailed discussion (chapter 6) on the value of the organizational structure of the French East India Company shows that the central policy of the Company's operation was determined by the Chamber of Directors in Paris, which was to be implemented by the Superior Council in Pondicherry for India operating through the Provincial Councils (as in Chandernagore in Bengal). The latter, in turn, supervised the subordinate factories under their command. As Munshi has shown, Chandernagore exploiting its geographical advantage with its proximity to the main political and commercial centres of Bengal – Hooghly, Kasimbazar, Malda and Murshidabad – and proper communication network, was able to make a sizeable profit during the period 1725-42 through its subordinate factories strategically located in Balasore, Kasimbazar, Patna, Dhaka and Jugdia.

Further, institutional corruption, as in the case of the English East India Company's attempt to establish a monopoly on salt, severely affected the English commercial interests.

Arijita Manna's richly-detailed work (chapter 8) has shown that the salt monopoly of the Company was a 'doomed enterprise'. Institutional weaknesses, the persistence of local trading systems, resistance from indigenous communities and unclear boundaries of the early colonial state – despite serious attempts at boundary maintenance – together ensured that large-scale smuggling of salt continued through various trade-routes intersected by water bodies, channels and forests. The Marathas, Arakan rulers, French Company officials and local interested parties worked in connivance with corrupt English Company employees for 'illicit' trade in salt, produced and marketed through a network not controlled by the state.

Besides, as Sayako Kanda (chapter 9) has analysed, the choice of a food item or any consumption material (in this case, salt) represented cultural, political and ritual values and, accordingly, shaped consumer preferences and the market. Price was important, and quality equally mattered. Salt was the second-largest source of revenue for the English Company; it attempted to control its production and supply to maintain high prices, which meant banning not only internal outputs but also importing a cheaper quality of salt from outside. The monopoly worked with some difficulty; the demand and supply of different varieties of salt – such as *panga* and *karkatch* – varied in different regions as per the taste of consumers. Some preferred the illegally-supplied, and low-priced *karkatch* to the costlier and refined salt sold in the market.

Other commodities, such as raw silk, had a different trajectory. Competition from Indian merchants catering to the traditional Asian demand for raw silk meant that the Bengali peasants involved in its production had a better negotiating capacity and hence, the English East India Company could not establish its monopoly on the silk trade. Roberto Davini (chapter 11) has made an interesting comparison of the ambitious introduction of Piedmontese reeling technology to produce silk in two British colonies, Georgia and Bengal, during the period 1730-1830. The Georgia experiment was a big disaster as despite everything they did – recruiting and training mulberry cultivators, silkworm-rearers, spinners and reelers, and paying them high salaries – the labour force refused to work. The abundance of fertile land and the scarcity of human resources meant that the landowners were able to secure more profit from cultivating staple crops like rice and indigo by exploiting unskilled labour. In contrast, the Company state drastically altered the traditional Bengali reeling technology to increase the sales of raw silk through the introduction of the Piedmontese reeling machine for better control of the production process. From the point of view of the Company, the experiment was satisfactory for vast quantities of low-quality raw silk were produced between the 1770s and the 1830s. Yet as the quality of silk was low, the idea of producing high-quality Piedmontese silk at a low cost was defeated.

The English East India Company state's attempts to optimize profits in areas under its control through the introduction of several new policies had disastrous consequences for traditional economic arrangements, especially those involving the peasants. Amrita Sengupta has illustrated (Chapter 15) how certain parts of Bengal, especially between 1779 and 1800, witnessed severe upheavals, including an insurgency by the Dashnami *sannyasi*s and Madariya *faqir*s in north Bengal, the Dhing peasant rebellion at Rangpore and the Chuar Adivasi disturbances in southern Bengal. The Company state not only resumed the rent-free land-grants that *sannyasi-faqir* institutions like the *maths* had enjoyed in several northern districts but also imposed curbs on their movement – pilgrimages and processions. These groups, which had access to considerable military resources created havoc in north Bengal for close to thirty years. The British succeeded, though not uniformly, in destroying the local-level political economy and culture in certain pockets by the late eighteenth century, which was resisted but without success.

The changes would be manifest not only in the late eighteenth-century political and economic sphere but in the cultural arena as well. This is captured in the portrayal or imaging in the eighteenth-century Murshidabad paintings. As Mrinalini Sil has shown (chapter 7), the courts of the Murshidabad *nawab*s were grand, displaying elaborate rituals with coded meanings, which were recorded in contemporary accounts and visually depicted in multiple paintings. The city of Murshidabad provided a platform for extraordinarily varied styles of art to emerge from the many interconnected painting traditions of the eighteenth century.

As politics changed from the Nizamat to the Company rule, noticeable changes were beginning to be felt in many aspects of life from the latter half of the eighteenth century. Natasha Eaton has presented (chapter 16) a fine art-historical analysis of the 'rubbishing' of Hindu deities, using a concept significantly termed as 'iconoclash', that is, a position somewhere between iconophilia and iconophobia – involving the extraordinary career of Charles 'Hindoo' Stuart, on the one hand, and the iconoclastic London Missionary Society missionaries, on the other. As Eaton elucidates, 'Unlike Company offcials who acquired Hindu images through theft, gift, prize or looting', missionary collections 'entailed rhetoric of legitimization – a theory of rubbish and of extraction of the sacred from places they could not enter (shrines, temples, elite homes)'. Even as the missionaries could get some local allies in their antagonism to idolatry and the partial conversion and secularization of idols through their transfer to museums in London, the controversial idol chamber of Colonel Stuart, which housed a large collection of images of various deities accumulated over half a century with the Colonel rumoured to be a worshipper of idols, sabotaged the efforts of the evangelical missionaries. His Calcutta home was eventually taken over by the London Missionary Society and cleansed of the numerous 'horrible' idols. Eaton, however, notes how Stuart had the last laugh as his 'will specified that the black basalt archway from a Shaiva Temple of the Pala period, a miniature temple, two statues of the river goddesses Ganga riding on a *makara* (crocodile) and Yamuna on a tortoise, a dome resembling the *amalaka* of an ancient Hindu temple and a lintel featuring the face of Shiva be incorporated into his colossal tomb at South Park Street, Calcutta', thus violating a Christian and deistic space with his idolatrous proclivities.

Though the Company sepoys and officials were able to neutralize cultic figures, there was confusion and a lack of clarity over such matters involving popular religious beliefs, and when they sought to intervene, they usually messed it up. The indigenous society had accommodated many local deities in Brahmanical religious rituals. The *mangalkavya* texts, composed between the fifteenth and eighteenth centuries, had made sense of popular religiosity, especially around the goddesses. Swarnali Biswas' study (chapter 13) refers to three well-known compositions – *Manasamangal*, *Chandimangal* and *Dharmamangal* – and attempts to see how women, both divine and human, were depicted in them. The narratives accord considerable power to goddesses such as Manasa and Chandi but, eventually, they are shown to be subordinated and domesticated by a male authority, such as the powerful male gods of the Hindu pantheon – for instance, Shiva as Manasa's father and Chandi's consort.

Since these are vernacular literary compositions of a religious or mythical nature, how do we deal with questions of corroboration with conventional sources used by previous generations of historians? A number of historians working on religious practices and historical traditions in medieval and early modern India have shown the way. The vernacular archive does provide considerable information on religious practices. In his study of accounts sheets, referred to as 'books of religion', Samuel Wright (chapter 10) relies almost entirely on this 'regional archive' to unravel complex practices of consumption among households and institutions organizing religious activities in eighteenth- and early nineteenth-century Bengal. The activities were varied and included *puja*s, household ceremonies, installations of idols and inauguration of monasteries. As Wright notes, the movement of goods and people depended upon multiple networks operating simultaneously. The accounts of expenses borne under different heads – from payments to Brahmins and helpers to specific amounts spent on things supplied with labour charges – were maintained in exact terms down to the last penny. The history of these practices in all their precision can be traced from, at least, the seventeenth century.

Further, as Ananya Roy Choudhury has shown in her article (chapter 14) on the early years of institutionalization of Bengali Vaishnavism, Hindu mobilization maintained an ambiguity on caste or *jati*-based hierarchy. Indeed, resisting Islam's dominant presence, Chaitanya identified Kaliyuga as the time when Brahmins would behave like Muslims. Accounts also refer to the confrontation of Chaitanya and his followers with a *qazi* and their subsequent reconciliation. Chaitanya and a group of Vaishnavas confronted a Muslim *qazi* who wanted to stop the *kirtana* and other Vaishnava religious gatherings.

The Sufi approach, in such contexts, was different, eclectic and pluralist, though located within the broader Islamic traditions. In the cosmopolitan background of seventeenth-century Arakan, ruled by the Buddhist dynasty of Marak U and boasting of a multilingual culture connected with the Indian Ocean network, the seventeenth-century Qadiri Sufi poet, Alaol, showed the way through his interesting strategy of diffusing several important Islamic cultural texts into the Bengali environment. Anwesha Sengupta's rich discussion (chapter 12) of Alaol's Bengali rendering of the Sufi poet Malik Muhammad Jaysi's famous Hindi *premakhyan*, *Padmavat*, written a century earlier, shows the interesting ways in which the poet dealt with the problem of translation. An attempt at a mere literal translation of a complex text could have been a meaningless exercise and departing entirely from it would not have done justice to the original. Hence, as Sengupta has shown through her close comparison of the prologue of the two versions, the original Hindi and its Bengali adaptation, Alaol's translation is not only a sincere reflection of the original text but also an in-depth interpretation, which he was able to achieve through an attempt at understanding the inner dynamics of the text. This was an important exercise as part of the effort to explain the complex Perso-Arabic Islamic discourse in the Bengali vernacular through the significant deployment of equivalent terms and phrases from the Sufi-*bhakti* milieu of the period.

Some fine studies on Sufism in medieval and early modern India have come up in recent decades, but Bengali Sufism is still attracting some historians to unpack a whole gamut of themes and issues involving Sufi activities from as early as the beginning of the thirteenth century. Some interesting works have come up from time to time, yet some pressing questions related to Sufis' political and cultural roles, such as their involvement in the diffusion and expansion of Islam, require more in-depth discussions. The Chishti Sufis of the Bengal Sultanate carried forward the traditions and practices adopted by their predecessors in Delhi, though important figures like Shaikh Akhi Siraj-ud-Din (d. 1357) and his successor (*khalifa*) in the Chishti lineage, Shaikh 'Ala-ul-Haq (d. 1398) did not maintain a critical distance from the political regime. Subsequently, 'Ala-ul-Haq's *khalifa*s, Syed Ashraf Jahangir Simnani (d. 1405) and Shaikh Nur Qutb-i-'Alam (d. 1415), are known to have played an active role in politics, influencing the Sultans of Jaunpur and Bengal, respectively. They are particularly remembered for their efforts to 'save' Islam from the sedition (*fasad*) of the mighty Hindu *zamindar*, Raja Ganesh, who had captured power to declare himself as the Sultan in his own right. Even though the *raja* would have made friendly gestures towards the custodians of Islam, his name could not have been read in the *khutba* (sermons) in the mosque. They resorted to an interesting way out of the crisis, with the *raja*'s son formally embracing Islam and styling as Sultan Jalal-ud-Din bin Raja Ganesh.

There is a need to explore some of the key issues relating to the emergence of Islam in Bengal and to understand the processes in the making of such a huge Bengali-speaking Muslim population. The early inroads of the Turkish conquerors in the thirteenth century, establishment of the Bengal Sultanate, arrival of the Sufis and their complex negotiations with the existing religious traditions, integration of Bengal as a Mughal *suba* (province), slow and gradual process of cultural accretion and Islamization, the question of identity formation, linguistic and religious attachments, and more recent issues of communal antagonism and neo-Islamic assertions require careful investigation.

Using a wide array of sources, the contributors of this volume, coming from diverse academic affiliations, and including several young researchers, have attempted to address historiographical shortcomings by deploying new material and offering fresh interpretations. Early modern Bengal's history does get overshadowed by later developments of the nineteenth century. What these assortments of articles highlight is that this period needs to be studied afresh.

To conclude with P.J. Marshall's endorsement in his Foreword to the book:

> What this volume clearly demonstrates is that the early modern history of Bengal is now studied by a much

wider range of people from a much greater diversity of institutions throughout the world than was the case in the 1960s. It, therefore, reflects trends that are general among the global historical community. The great political and economic narratives of subjection and impoverishment are presumably taken for granted. They have given way to a mass of highly suggestive insights into the trade, politics and culture of Bengal, which show that whatever the outside pressures may have been, the Bengali people made their own history. This rich collection leaves no doubt that the historiography of Bengal is currently in very capable hands.

[Based on my Introduction to Raziuddin Aquil and Tilottama Mukherjee (eds.), *An Earthly Paradise: Trade, Politics and Culture in Early Modern Bengal*, with a Foreword by P.J. Marshall, New Delhi: Manohar, 2020.]

24

ONE THOUSAND YEARS OF BENGALI CULTURE

GHULAM MURSHID's book, *Bengali Culture over a Thousand Years*, was originally written for 'intelligent non-academic' Bengali readers and published from Dhaka in 2006. Sarbari Sinha has offered a fine translation which reads like an original piece of work. In her Translator's Note, Sinha has beautifully summed up the purpose and value of this work in the troubled times we inhabit. She writes:

> Almost everywhere in the world, the walls are growing taller and more rigid as people turn away from history and ignore narratives that speak of shared destinies. More than ever before, this is the time to tell and share stories on the basis of recorded history instead of hearsay and social myths. If histories do not come out of the confines of academia and become part of everyday conversations, myth-making and bigotries inevitably usurp the intellectual space that is left vacant.

Ghulam Murshid's work emerges from radio programmes and newspaper columns, where they were first offered to a large public interested to know about the history and culture of the Bengali people over the past thousand years. On closer look, it would appear that Bengal as a region, Bangla language, and Bengali people we know have emerged with distinct cultural markers during the past six-seven centuries, though the pre-history of literary traditions, cultural practices and geographical formations in the region identified as parts of greater river-washed Bengal can go back another couple of centuries or more. In all, a thousand years sound good for the rise of the Bengalis!

Spread over 14 chapters, 644 pages in all, the voluminous book covers a whole gamut of themes on the cultural history of Bengal. Defining Bengali-speaking and fish-and-rice eating people as Bengalis, despite differences and difficulties of different kinds – region, religion, caste (despite the apparent lack of it) and rural-urban divide – the author has, as is generally the case, sought endorsement from the venerable Rabindranath Tagore. The latter is quoted as saying:

> The history of Bengal is the history of fragmentation. Eastern and western Bengal, Rarh and Varendra, these are not simply geographical divisions; divisions of hearts and minds were meshed up with them, and social unity was also absent. Yet through it all there runs a strain of unity, and that is the unity of language. What defines us as being Bengali is that we happen to speak Bengali.

And, this is not accidental. A long history of cultural investment has made a Bengali *adda* a Bengali *adda*! This can only be maintained through a deliberate distinction between a Bengali and non-Bengali, even though the latter might learn to speak the language, with varying proficiency and accents. Language sophistication then is an important marker, which also distinguishes an inhabitant from a *probashi* (expatriate). When language is taken care of religion takes over. As it does with religion in contemporary West Bengal: Hindus have appropriated Bengali identity for themselves; for them, Muslims are Muslims, even if they are Bengali-speaking. Bengali Muslims themselves have struggled with their dual identity – Bengali and Muslim – with terrible consequences in their history. To be a Bengali by birth and language, therefore, is a carefully-crafted identity.

The well-meaning Bengali scholars have always tried to rise above political divisions to emphasize the value of shared cultural practices – encompassing east and west Bengal as well as religious divides, variations between the rural and urban people, besides class differences between *bhadralok* and *chhotolok* (though the latter are not explicitly identified as such). The unfinished business of the making of Bengali identity of the tribals, or *adivasis*, who are not perceived as properly Bengali, in terms of their cultural sophistication, also remains a problem. All these have led to complex processes of appropriations and exclusions which have made Bengali culture what it is.

After a short chapter on the beginning of the antecedents of what constitutes Bengali culture, Murshid appropriately turns to the cultural transformations in the Indo-Muslim era, drawing attention to nearly 550 years of a sort of indirect 'Muslim rule' in Bengal, from early-thirteenth to mid-eighteenth centuries. The Muslim rulers came down from different parts of Central and West Asia. They spoke different languages and did not belong to a monolithic culture. Though they had a common religious identity, they had not 'travelled to Bengal to preach Islam or to establish Islamic rule'. Arabic, Persian and Turkish-speaking Muslim immigrants brought with themselves 'varied cultural and civilizational traits of a vast region of the globe' and over centuries also underwent considerable mutations through marriage with local women, beginning the process of becoming a Bengali Muslim. This was similar to north Indian Brahmin immigrants marrying Santhal women to form the process of the making of Bengali Brahmins, even though it might sound scandalous to those with no or little sense of history.

The intermingling between Muslim rulers and nobles of central Islamic lands on the one hand and local intermediaries on the other, besides 'Bengalicization' of the immigrants, left clear marks on religion, architecture, literature and various other aspects of culture. The use of bricks and terracotta designs gave a distinct character to Islamic architecture in Bengal with mosques, *mazar*s and *dargah*s with all their domes, minarets and arches beginning to dot the spiritual landscape. In this and several other features, one can see what Richard Eaton characterises as the 'double movement' in Bengal's Islamic traditions – Bengali and Islamic – which features will be privileged when would depend on the ethnic or religious politics of the time.

As Murshid wrote in the chapter on society and religion, the advent of Islam in the medieval period produced a process of opposition and assimilation between the local and the imported religions. This was similar to the kind witnessed earlier under rulers patronising strands of Vedic (Shaivite) and Buddhist (Sahajiya) forms of worship, in a context in which the local rural masses subscribed to a range of beliefs, invoked many gods and goddesses, and performed their rituals and *vrata*s (propitiation of folk deities, usually performed by women). Religious beliefs and practices in Bengal have, thus, acquired many influences to the extent that sometimes they just cannot be easily boxed into one religion or the other. Some such cases are often referred to as syncretism or syncretic sects, revealing accretions from a variety of sources. This would also mean that Islam or Hindu traditions in Bengali communities are not always the exact replicas of their sources. The Bengali interpretation and appropriation would make them something of their own, and thus a marker of their distinct identity. A Bengali Muslim will not be the same as a Bihari Muslim or a Punjabi for that matter, no degree of fundamentalism can, for long, dissolve the cultural markers which set them apart. Islam in Bengal, therefore, was going to have its distinct character.

The process of religious assimilation summed up by the author include the suggestion that Buddhism was influenced most by Tantric modes of worship, which in turn spawned several sects and branches through varied influences and incorporations. Further, as wives, daughters and daughters-in-law of Shiva, the non-Aryan goddesses became accepted as deities in the Hindu tradition. A variety of *mangalkavya*s has illustrated this process. Also, literature associated with Hindu revivalist movement around the figure of Chaitanyadev and his Vaishnava devotion revealed its resistance to the massive political presence of Islam. Faith in Bengal has always been devotional and inclined towards *guru*s (spiritual mentors and teachers). Not surprisingly, therefore, it was the non-dualistic, devotional and *guru*-dependent Islam that flourished in Bengal. Thus, a tradition of unceremonious and syncretic faith – triumphing over institutionalized religion – assimilated Buddhist Sahajiya ideals, the Sufi world view of Islam, and the stress on love in Vaishnavism; it drew even on Tantric beliefs and found soulful expression in the Bauls, who emerged as early as the fifteenth century. The latter sang the songs of love as a matter of the heart, moving away from the usual codified chants (*mantras*).

The distinctive qualities of its own mark many other aspects of Bengali culture across communities, sub-regions and centuries. Though Murshid has noticed the process of Persianization of Bengali literary tradition under the Mughals, beginning late in the sixteenth century, he has somewhat cryptically remarked that the conquerors could not make sense of the language, clothes and food of the Bengali people. The author wrote: 'These roti-and-meat-eating outsiders of the Mughal age detested the fish and rice of Bengal'. Whatever may be the truth, the other way assimilation is evident today: by most accounts the Mughlai in Calcutta, which is the Mecca of Bengali culture now, offers some of the best preparations of *kebab*, *chap* and *biryani* with their mouth-watering flavours catering to varied tastes, ranging from hot and spicy to mild and fragrant. If one has not tasted these, one is not properly introduced to either Mughlai or Bengali culinary culture. These are best prepared by professional cooks (*bawarchis*) working for ubiquitous restaurants. In older times, one could lose caste by eating rotis or smelling meat, but since nineteenth century those who sought to defy taboos jumped college walls for beef-*kebab*!

Further, as someone claiming to be not bound to any national or ethnic identity, Murshid claims in his chapter on food culture: 'People of many other provinces of India, however, do not view this fish-eating habit of Bengalis too kindly. Many people in the subcontinent still do not eat fish.'

Noting that historical records 'reflect the love that the people of this land have for fish', the author quotes an early text: 'Fortunate is the man whose wife serves freshly cooked rice, clarified butter from cow's milk, leaves and gravy of sardines everyday on plantain leaves'. The author concludes: 'Bengali food has so far retained its own distinctiveness despite the many changes in food, drinks and modes of hospitality over the past 1,000 years'.

When we are into gastronomic delights and satisfaction, can we ignore a fine conversation on music, films and other art forms? Murshid has offered detailed discussion in dedicated chapters on all these. These constitute cultural capital of the Bengali people, with considerable investments going back to five centuries, if not ten. The tradition of *kirtan*, devotional songs sung by Gaudiya Vaishnavas, formed something of a unique school of music in the early modern era. Excellence in music in modern times can also be seen in the fusion of different kinds, often influenced by Western vocal and instrumental traditions.

The English-knowing Bengali clerk, the *babu*, had already appeared by the late eighteenth century, with Calcutta picking up English quickly, along with other markers of Western modernity. Many fields such as literature, theatre, films and other modern art forms manifested changes wrought by Western influence in different phases, from the early modern to colonial modern transformations and post-colonial changes.

All in all, great efforts were made to attain sophistication and excellence in several cultural fields – art forms and performance – together comprising the chequered cultural history of the region. Negative comments on the Bengalis, either as internal critique or perceptions of outsiders, include:

the tame, timid but well-mannered, lazy and idle Bengalis attached to the comforts of home and the *para* resemble the proverbial frog in the well. Such criticisms, as an 1885 one succinctly stated: 'Bengalis will starve to death at home and yet refuse to go out and look for food', should not detract from their cultural attainments.

When a book on this scale is written, some details might appear problematic for the specialists of different fields and eras of history, but the narrative as a whole captures the larger cultural contours. Since so many varied things have been discussed, a separate chapter on festivities would serve as an occasion to showcase the celebrations, cultural aesthetics and pleasures of life, as in the case of Durga Puja which is central to Bengali culture for over two centuries now. *Baro mashe tero parbon* (thirteen festivals in twelve months of the year), goes the popular Bengali saying and with good reason!

As is the usual practice, followed by Murshid also, we conclude with reference to Tagore's extraordinary internationalism and cosmopolitan outlook:

> In this age of communal disharmony and heightened cultural and religious identities, we will also do well to remember how Tagore's work inspired several generations of Hindu and Muslim Bengalis to draw closer on the basis of their shared linguistic identity. The ideal of a liberal, secular and humanist universalism that formed the underpinning of Tagore's work and his worldview continues to inspire progressive Bengalis today.

The author, translator and publisher deserve much appreciation for meticulously bringing out this huge volume covering many scintillating aspects of cultural history of Bengal.

[Review of Ghulam Murshid, *Bengali Culture Over a Thousand Years*, translated from the original Bengali, *Hajaar Bochhorer Bangla Samskriti* by Sarbari Sinha, New Delhi: Niyogi Books, 2018. Published in the *Frontline*, 1 February 2019. URL: https://frontline.thehindu.com/books/article26003781.ece?homepage=true.]

25

MODERN SOCIAL HISTORY AT ITS BEST

THE BEST OF histories are produced in the worst of times. Distinguished scholars rise above aggressive political propaganda to publish historical works providing critical insights on what happened in the past – some lessons from which can shape the present. One such historian, the much admired Professor Sumit Sarkar has devoted his life working with just one agenda – scholarly excellence. In doing so, he has questioned received wisdom, pushed disciplinary boundaries, and set high standards of critical historical thinking. His formidable scholarship can be savoured in his recently published book, *Essays of a Lifetime: Reformers, Nationalists, Subalterns* (Permanent Black). Offering Bengal's modern social history at its best, the book's blurb highlights: 'The present collection, which reproduces many of Sarkar's finest writings, shows an intellectually scintillating, sceptical-Marxist mind at its sharpest'.

Spread over 640 pages, the book is divided into three sections. The first part comprising eight chapters offers a detailed critique of the contradictory pulls of social reform and religious revival in colonial Bengal. Humiliation of colonial subjugation was to be balanced with glorification of India's ancient past and attack on the so-called tyranny and oppression of Muslim rule before the British conquest. This meant even the most sincere of reform efforts falling prey to what was subsequently identified as the infamous divide-and-rule policy of the British, besides capitulating to the contradictions between traditional norms and modern transformations. The second set of six chapters further reveals Sarkar's long engagement with various strands of subaltern activism and nationalist interventions, as the foremost scholar of Swadeshi movement in Bengal with a lapsed association with critical Subaltern Studies scholarship of the 1980s and 1990s. The third section offers rich tributes to eminent scholars and activists P.C. Joshi, Eric Hobsbawm and E.P. Thompson, with Sarkar acknowledging his intellectual debt especially to the latter.

Some of the themes and issues of crucial import to the history of Bengal and by extension of rest of India may be highlighted here. In a provocative opening chapter in which conclusions are offered upfront, Sarkar points out that Raja Rammohun Roy's writings and activities signify a break with tradition, but a close investigation of the precise extent and nature of the departure reveals it was constrained by a Hindu-elitist and colonial framework. The much touted Bengal renaissance, therefore, was an intellectual movement of a 'false consciousness of pathetic kind', which was bred by colonialism. Beyond laudatory rhetoric, it did not lead to basic social transformation in a progressive direction in Bengal's development, which, indeed, saw a break from the level-playing field of early modern era to 'the full blast of colonial modern exploitation'.

The march to modernity eventually slid into conformity to caste rules to the extent of Rammohun taking a Brahmin cook with him to England, wearing sacred threads to the end of his days, hunting for texts glorifying ascetic widowhood even if for the noble intention of countering *sati*, and other deeply flawed actions revealing contradictions in theory and practice. In effect, it meant complete abandonment of the older Persianate-Islamic intellectual framework to embrace a neo-Hindu revivalism induced by almost a blind acceptance of colonial subjection. These limits, contradictions, and ambivalence are not taken into consideration in usual celebration of Rammohun as the father of modern India. Yet, it must be recognised that it took nearly a century-long reform-struggle to eventually banish *sati* and allow widow-remarriage.

As Sarkar succinctly puts it, the Hindu tradition always combines 'a very considerable degree of abstract intellectual freedom with insistence upon rigid social conformity, and Rammohun and the early Brahmos on the whole maintained this dichotomy'. The challenge posed by the contemporaneous Derozians (pupils and friends of early nineteenth-century avant-garde poet and public intellectual Henri Louis Vivian Derozio) through their open rejection of rituals and defiance of caste and religious taboos was alarming. They began with radical new lifestyle and free thinking, and were condemned for 'cutting their way through ham and beef, and wading to liberalism through tumblers of bear'. However, as Sarkar shows in his discussion on the complexities of 'Young Bengal' movement, the youthful exuberance of modern educated college boys eventually succumbed to the pressures of newly articulated Hindu conservatism of colonial Bengal.

Within a few decades, Derozian reading groups and societies were seen conforming to the prejudices of the time, with little to show for any radical departure in thinking about religion and philosophy. On the questions of social reform also – the need for education, evils of child-marriage and Kulin polygamy, parental arrangement of marriages, seclusion of women, and ban on widow-remarriage – the Derozians maintained varied positions from ambiguities to 'backsliding'. Sarkar has particularly noted, with a tinge of sadness, the attack on the alleged cruelty of precolonial Muslim rule, which was represented as the reason for seclusion of women, whereas the Hindu Shastras were not so conservative, it was held. The colonial rule was celebrated as delivering from Muslim oppression; the haughty, wretched and oppressive Yavanas were being driven out and it was hoped that public jobs will be denied to them once Persian was deprived of its court language status. They also raised a false alarm on the suppression of Bengali language and literature under Muslim rulers, but called for the vernacular to be taught only to the *raiyat* children in district schools, emphasizing on English education to be reserved for rich upper-caste/ *zamindar* kids in schools and colleges. Thus, in many ways, the so-called radicals were not much different from the moderates or even the conservatives, despite all the heavy drinking which made them appear iconoclastic.

In Sarkar's analysis, the social-reform issues threw up four distinct positions: secular reform of the Vidyasagar brand, agnostic, atheist, steering clear of religious ideologies and working for social engineering, even if piecemeal; Brahmoism, at the height of its influence in 1860s and 1870s, declining rapidly thereafter; the positivist circles; and the rising tide of Hindu revival. All of them converged on 'all-pervading assumption that British rule had been preceded by centuries of Muslim tyranny and therefore had to be welcomed as a deliverance from an age of darkness'. From Rammohun and the Derozians, to Keshabchandra, Bankimchandra and a host of conservatives and progressives alike suffered from this 'ubiquitous syndrome' throughout nineteenth-century Bengal. As Sarkar puts it:

> A break had taken place with pre-nineteenth-century Indo-Islamic culture through the displacement of Persian by English, and more generally by the myth of the 'renaissance' itself, for awakening has to presuppose a dark age.

This was bound to snowball into a communal conflagration and divide in decades to come, when poor Muslim peasants began to revolt against rich Hindu zamindars (at it happens, using the language of political Islam and *jihad*).

The interesting 'sequence of significant effort and ultimate failure', often returning to status quo ante, though sometimes witnessing lasting shifts as well, has been studied by Sarkar further with reference to the political domain, especially pattern and structure of nationalist activity in Bengal. The 'zig-zag pattern of nationalist activity' is examined within the emerging structure of nationalism – 'the entire complex of objectives, techniques, sociocultural ideals and values, organizational forms, communication media, and social composition which together make up the texture of a movement'. All things considered, 'the history of the Indian national movement reveals interesting crests followed by troughs'. The failure of both radical intellectual heroes and much exploited peasant rebels indicates the specific ways in which colonial situation warped, hindered, or frustrated legitimate aspirations. In Sarkar's words, 'the limitations of the intellectuals, radical and conservative alike, were connected with the socio-economic structure moulded by colonialism'. However, active collaboration or silent weeping eventually gave way to political action, preparing ground for developing a coherent ideology in the shape of drain of wealth theory.

Sarkar also presents a complex picture of the caste question, moving from simple binaries: religious-cum-caste relations complicated by class status, Muslim and Christian presence offering salvation, and Gandhi coming up with his own notions, though maintaining ambivalence on equality and social and scriptural justification of discrimination and hierarchy (*adhikarbhed*) in society. Combating this, marginalized, but politically assertive communities such as Namsudras, Mahishyas and Rajbansis came up with their own vernacular histories articulating their identities. Namsudras protested against being condemned as Chandals, for the latter were identified as descendants of a Brahmin woman producing children through sex with a Shudra man. Namsudras imagined themselves other way round and in a better position: descended from intercourse between a Shudra woman and a Brahmin sage. They sought to enhance their social respectability and political status through education, which was hitherto denied to them by upper-caste *bhadralok*s, who, indeed, according to reports, tried to prevent Namsudras from opening schools for educating their children.

Further, Mahishyas refused comparisons with Namsudras, pointing to upper castes having had water from their hands. That was the bottom line identified as: *jalacharanya*! Also, Rajbansi upper-crust claimed Kshatriya status, rejecting any connection with the tribal group Koch, purging their customs of 'non-Aryan' modes, and constructing a more prestigious history of the community. In doing so, Rajbansi leadership allied itself with upper-caste Hindu identity politics with an anti-Muslim slant. Mercifully, this kind of build up collapsed in the face of a class solidarity resulting in the Tebhaga movement of mid-1940s. Yet, the Marxian Left's understanding of caste as 'epiphenomenon of class' did not help either. The two registers of caste and class defused any possibility of a broad plank for transformative politics. Further, as Sarkar notes, solidarities based on nation, region, religion or community, class, caste, tribe or women are unable to sustain themselves beyond a point – making identities around them fluid and transient with multiple possibilities.

Working from within the emerging Hindu-fold, Ramakrishna Paramhansa (1836-86) warned his followers against falling in the usual trap of lust and greed which forced them to endure the humiliation of colonial government employment as lowly and depressed clerks (the troika of *kamini*, *kanchan* and *chakri*) – resembling conditions of Kaliyuga and calling for *avatars* or gods for course correction, sometimes with scandalous results. Sarkar's fascinating chapter on 'terrible immoralities', including ritual murder, terrifying arson and sexual perversion involving a self-styled Kalki *avatar* and his few disciples in a village of Bikrampur, reputed as a civilized heartland of Bengali Hindu *bhadralok*, is a case in point. This was a scandal that was to be hushed into silence, for it also had a Chandal or Namsudra character who was welcomed into a village Brahmin *bhadralok's* household in which women outnumbered men, only to completely violate established norms during a night-long orgy and violence in mid-December 1904. The term Kalki was also abused by the *sadhus*, who used it for calling the penis-shaped pipe for smoking *ganja*, which, in turn, could give a heady feeling of setting things right side up again. There were other uses made of both the ashes and the pipe itself.

From a more sensible context, though sometimes charged with emotions bordering on madness, Sarkar quotes *Ramakrishna Kathamrita* in which the Guru (Ramakrishna Paramhansa) articulated the catholicity of traditional and inclusive Hinduism, recognizing many separate ways to achieve the same goal:

> There is a pond with three or four *ghat*s – Hindus call what they drink *jal*, Muslims *pani*, the English water. He is called Allah by one, God by others, some say Brahma, others Kali, still others Ram, Hari, Jesus, or Durga.

The Bengali *bhadralok's* urbanity was carefully shaped in the nineteenth century by an intelligent mix of tradition and modernity, which was aimed at transcending the narrow limits of the usual caste and religion based prejudices, though in some contexts its lapsing into politics of Hindutva kind cannot be ruled out altogether. The considerable sophistication provided to a broad-based Hinduism by Swami Vivekananda, a renowned successor of Ramakrishna, is susceptible to misuse for narrow political ends in our time.

Sarkar offers interesting insights on these important issues. Broadly following the same tradition of scholarship of Thompsonian social history kind and maintaining critical historical distance, Professor Neeladri Bhattacharya writes in his endorsement on the back cover: Sumit Sarkar critiques his own location within the new Marxist nationalist history –

'pushing disciplinary boundaries, disturbing neat classifications, resisting false historical comparisons, problamatizing categories, and questioning linear narratives'. The end product is awe-inspiring scholarship presented in the gentlest of form and style. Sarkar doesn't need to shout like political ideologues and propagandists. He commands respect for the outstanding research he has done and meticulously produced books he has published.

[A shorter version of this write-up has appeared in the *Sunday Guardian*: https://www.sundayguardianlive.com/opinion/modern-social-history-best.]

26

UNPACKING THEORY AND HISTORY IN A DIALOGIC RELATIONSHIP

AT A TIME WHEN reports of all kinds of deliberate attempts to destroy Jawaharlal Nehru University, one of the leading universities especially of the liberal arts in India, are rife, one of its finest historians, Professor Neeladri Bhattacharya has again reminded us why it is rated so highly in academia. His pathbreaking monograph on significant transformations in Punjab under British rule (1849-1947) adds to his legendary reputation of a teacher par excellence in Centre for Historical Studies for over four decades. Much admired for his enthralling lectures on problems of historical writing and method, Professor Bhattacharya would never cease to mesmerize through his grounding in both grand theories, as well as empirical details, the touchstone of the historian's craft.

In the book, as in his lectures, Professor Bhattacharya has grappled with dominant ideologies, fashionable theories, colonial archives and the crucial agrarian questions in Punjab and elsewhere. Assumptions and ideologies can be set aside if they do not further our understanding – thus underlining the tensions between theory and history. Even theories and categories are interrogated and modified. These are methodological concerns not only for understanding colonial India, with undivided Punjab as a test case but also for pre-colonial or Mughal history as well as later political conflicts and crises. The central concern in his book is to trace the colonial conquest and transformations through administrative measures, archival records and responses on the grounds.

The aggressive and deep British penetration meant old-style paternal benevolent governance was discarded to establish an authoritarian regime, with tenancies, tenures, properties, and habitations brought under control through new administrative apparatus and law-courts. This involved systematically mapping, classifying, categorizing, demarcating fields, planning irrigation, introducing crops and trees, clearing scrubs, and restricting access to the commons. The social engineering by the colonial state which produced the colonial agrarian order could be seen in meticulous maintenance of records, manuals, settlement papers, village maps, boundaries, etc. All these were brought under the jurisdiction of the evolving laws, covering property acts, codes of customs, rules of inheritance, and tenancy rights.

These changes had broad ramifications, which affected many aspects of life in the rural world, agrarian and non-agrarian. Murmurs of protest were eventually bound to irrupt into an open movement for independence and freedom. The notions of pre-colonial abundance, prosperity, peace, and freedom were pitched against widespread poverty, debt, litigation, high prices and taxation under colonial rule. The future *azadi* was contrasted with the present slavery, which had left the country in tatters. The ruptures were so deep that even well-meaning British observers dismissed genuine grievances as blatant lies. The early belief in British benevolent paternalism had come to a cropper, with aggressive authoritarianism leading to terrible consequences, although officials lived in denial.

The Pax Britannica was presented as synonymous with a prosperous, progressive and modern society, which was contrasted with the nomadic, primitive, and fatalistic world view of the colonized, needing enlightenment. By the end of the British rule, the lament was: 'We have nothing to eat, we are dying of hunger, there is no sugar, no cloth, no matches. Look at our children, how ravaged they are. Our lot is unbearable.'

The much-celebrated canal colony completely shattered the traditional ecological balance, with pastoralists barred from the jungles, thus destroying their livelihoods and even food habits. On the other hand, continuous waterlogging and frequent floods in the villages along the great canal network made life unbearable; villages had to be abandoned, as the land was destroyed by salinity and malaria wreaked havoc.

Complete subversion of the existing systems and subjugation of people was the foundational aim of colonial conquest. Colonialism and imperialism had no redeeming features. In British perception of its rule, the beginning was marked by promises of a better future, and it ended with disavowal and rejection. Peace, justice and enough to eat would be possible with *azadi* from colonial slavery is what the people hoped. And, as is the case with all desperate regimes in India, the British played the Hindu-Muslim card until the last months of their departure.

Professor Bhattacharya's voluminous work, spread over 500 pages, and divided into ten chapters in four sections, besides a concise historiographical introduction and a conclusion referring to colonial nostalgia in the months leading to Independence, offers stimulating and valuable insights on a whole range of themes and issues in the history of colonial India. In the distinguished historian's words: the attempt is to unpack the nitty-gritty of theory and history in a 'dialogic' relationship – which he does with admirable finesse.

[Based on Professor Neeladri Bhattacharya's book, *The Great Agrarian Conquest: The Colonial Reshaping of a Rural World*, published by Permanent Black, 2018. Published in the *Sunday Guardian*: https://www.sundayguardianlive.com/news/unpacking-theory-history-dialogic-relationship.]

27

READING THE *GULISTAN* OF SA'DI SHIRAZI

IF MUSLIMS RULED in medieval India reading classical Persian texts, the British colonial administrators also wanted to learn to read and learn from them, though the pre-colonial regimes were to be condemned for presiding over a dark age from which they claimed the country was being liberated by them. Thus, translations of Persian classics was a part of the agenda as was the attempt to learn languages such as Persian, Sanskrit and the regional vernaculars. Certainly, Persian needed to be learned as the then language of power and also Sanskrit to discover ancient Hindu traditions. Some of these efforts eventually went on to create a huge crisis in Indian society – in terms of intervention in traditional practices and hardening of sectarian or communal identities.

The English translation of Sa'di's *Gulistan* by Major R.P. Anderson was published in 1861 by Thacker Spink and Co., Calcutta, which is well known for publication of a number of 'Oriental' works. Major Anderson worked in the Lucknow Garrison of the English East India Company army and has dedicated his translation, which he calls 'Analysis', to Sir Henry Lawrence, who died during the siege of Lucknow in 1857. Anderson writes in his Introduction that he was contributing to the cause of 'the good of the government'.

He added that 'every person should endeavour to add what *little* he can to the general stock of Oriental literature' (emphasis original). For, he noted, 'there can be no "justice" till Europeans fully understand the language of the natives of India'. It was, therefore, announced on the title page that the text was prepared by the author purely to facilitate the study of the Persian language.

Mentioning that the older English translation of *Gulistan* by Francis Gladwin (d. *c.*1813) was available to him, Anderson explains that his attempt was to offer a fresh translation as key to learn and grasp faster – reducing the period of mastering the *Gulistan* by 'full one-fourth, if not more'. Gladwin was one of the founding members of the Asiatic Society, Calcutta, and also served as a professor of Persian at Fort William College, Calcutta, since its establishment in the year 1800. His English translation of Sa'di's *Gulistan* was published with the original text in two volumes from Calcutta in 1806. He was already well known for his translations of Persian classics, including the foremost Mughal text, which the new British rulers needed to master, Abu'l Fazl's *A'in-e Akbari* (*Ayeen Akbery or The Institutes of Emperor Akbar*, published from London, between 1783-6).

In offering a fresh translation of *Gulistan*, Anderson did not mean any disrespect to the older translator, Gladwin, who earlier worked for the same cause. Deploying the metaphor of innumerable ships traversing the ocean, Anderson writes:

> although ships conveying the *same* description of cargo may eventually reach their destination, still a merchant *prefers* the one that will reach the haven the *soonest*. So also with translations, all may be 'substantially correct',

> but some require 'less time' to understand (emphasis original).

Anderson has also mentioned that he has attempted to show 'the depth and beauty of thought' of the elegant and inimitable Persian master who, according to him, has not been sufficiently commended for his 'transcendant abilities and lofty powers of imagination'. He has also informed that as a translator he has strictly adhered to the original, being accurate – adding nothing, omitting nothing. Though he had taken the help of 'Natives', who apparently did not understand a word of English, Anderson claimed his translation was an original endeavour, invoking Sa'di: 'It is better to wear your own tattered garments than to bossom your neighbour's coat (*kuhan khirqah khweesh pairaastan, beh az jaameh-e 'ariyat khwaastan*)'. This was derived from the concluding part of *Gulistan* in which Sa'di has asserted that the fine poetry given by him throughout the book was his own composition, noting somewhat sarcastically that he had not followed the usual custom of authors inserting verses borrowed from former writers (*rasm muwallifaan az sh'er mutaqaddemaan be-tariq iste'areh talfiqi na-raft*).

The amazing amount of hard work that Anderson has put in can be seen from the fact that every word in Sa'di's original Persian text has been numbered. Below the text, nearest English equivalents are given against the number for a particular Persian word. These words are then brought together in a sentence to offer a coherent meaning of the original. In cases where literal meanings of words do not convey what the poet meant to say, the translator has revised the part and printed it in italics – in a bid to express the full sense of the original, but 'never to amplify or exaggerate'. The original publisher, Thacker Spink and Co., also deserve commendation for undertaking such a remarkable project of the kind rarely seen in our time despite all the technological advances in typesetting and printing.

[Based on my Introduction to: Major R.P. Anderson, *The Gulistan of Shaikh Sa'di Shirazi* (Originally published as *The Gulistan of Shaik Saday: A Complete Analysis of the Entire Persian Text*), Calcutta: Thacker Spink and Co., 1861, reprint, New Delhi: Manohar, 2020.]

28

HISTORIES OF TRIBALS AND DALITS

BOOKS ARE BANNED and burnt in persecuting societies and oppressive regimes. Scholars and writers giving voice to the dispossessed and disenfranchized come within the ambit of what is identified as questioning the power and legitimacy of the state and, thus, misunderstood as seditious. However, this does not deter those firmly committed to the rights of the marginal groups at the wrong side of power relations in a hierarchical social structure under a feudal or capitalistic political order. The Oxford University Press deserves commendation for publishing the richly argued work of historian Biswamoy Pati posthumously, on the forbidding history of horrendous social exclusion of tribals, untouchables, low-caste people and the landless rural poor in the highlands of western Orissa (now Odisha), in districts bordering Jharkhand and Chhattisgarh. These people were sought to be invisibilized in history and marginalized in dominant political discourse. Biswamoy Pati's work starts *c.* 1800 and closes in 1950, amidst massive social and political upheavals of decolonization, Independence and the making of the modern Indian state. The work is of crucial import as the struggles for survival of these people have continued since Independence.

The coastal pilgrim town of Puri with Lord Jagannath

emerging as the presiding deity, the princely states of Kalahandi and Mayurbhanj are among the major sites in Orissa – comprising coastal eastern district plains and the mineral rich western hilly region – which witnessed horrid 'rhythms of change and devastation' caused by colonial capitalism. Traditional arrangements, even if of pre-colonial feudal kind, of control and use of land were disrupted by frequent measurement and accordingly increased revenue demands, which were referred to as settlements. New forest laws almost entirely barred tribal population from using its resources on which they had hitherto depended for subsistence. Denuding forests in the name of infrastructural development and industry was a common practice, leading to large-scale displacement with no arrangements for proper rehabilitation. The social and religious transformations witnessed an aggressive process of Brahmanization and Oriyaization in which tribals were placed at the lower order of caste and class hierarchy. In other words, the traditions, customs, rituals and, indeed, the very livelihood of people identified as Adivasis, as also Dalits, were shattered.

These much-exploited people hit back against feudal chiefs of princely states, who had themselves possibly undergone a process of Kshatriyaization from their tribal origins before claiming Rajput status. They relentlessly defied the fast-expanding tentacles of British exploitative colonial regime. The emerging Oriya middle class, fashioning itself into Sanskritik Brahmanical Hinduism combined with a deceptively hypocritical Western colonial modernity, which the representatives of the competitive Lutheran and Roman Catholic missions could not handle properly, was also questioned. The whole of the nineteenth and first half of the twentieth centuries would, thus, see tribal population continuously involved in resistance of everyday kind (using abusive or dismissive epithets, often in Hindi, to call out the oppressors), violent protest involving murder and bloodbath (sometimes making a ghastly spectacle of brutal lynching of a *zamindar*'s agent) and mocking dominant rituals of power and legitimacy (such as giving up on Hindu appropriation of tribal God, Jagannath and launching a new Mahima Dharma with its strong message of egalitarianism and humanism, moving away from scripturally sanctified social-stratification).

The political regime retaliated with all its might, with anecdotal accounts reporting massive crackdowns in which large numbers of tribal rebels were killed; communities which were on the forefront of resistance movements were targeted as criminal tribes and mercilessly brutalized. The state also made a mess of traditional notions of illness and methods of healing by introducing new Western medical practices, betraying a complete moral and intellectual bankruptcy in dealing with severely affecting diseases such as cholera, leprosy and mental disorders. Mentally ill were condemned as criminal lunatics, and poor lepers were quarantined. Emerging urban spaces were segregated between the posh enclaves for the rich and resourceful and poor settlements with little amenities for the downtrodden.

The pauperization of the tribals and their condemnation as lazy drunkards, coupled with the humiliation of dry fish consuming untouchables and beef-eating impoverished Muslims as carriers of leprosy virus, would mean large sections of the people were attacked for the condition they were forced to live in. The traditional political organizations such as the Kisan Sabha and Praja Mandals were in no position to ensure justice for the oppressed. Later interventions by leaders of the national movement and the Communists could not resolve the difficulties as they struggled with their contradictions, competitions and attempts to run down each other. This is the murky legacy that the modern Indian state has struggled to handle for over 70 years.

[Based on Biswamoy Pati, *Tribals and Dalits in Orissa: Towards a Social History of Exclusion, c.1800-1950*, Oxford University Press, 2019. Published in the *Sunday Guardian*: https://www.sundayguardianlive.com/news/light-shed-history-odishas-tribals-dalits.]

29

PARTITION'S BIHARIS: A TRIBUTE TO DR PAPIYA GHOSH

MY AIM HERE is to draw attention to Papiya Ghosh's significant research on the despicable history of separatism, violence and displacement of the Muslim minority population of 'Bihari' origin through the major part of the twentieth century. No other historian of Islam and Muslims in the Hindu majority province of Bihar and its adjoining areas, including parts of eastern UP, has been able to come up with a more synthetic account of the troublesome history of the community, with all its social stratifications and religious diversities (*ashraf/arzal*, Shia/Sunni, etc.).

It is also amazing to think that it was possible for Papiya Ghosh to work on this huge project from a place like Patna with no or little infrastructure and yet the results of her scholarship matches the best in the field. In fact, much of the standard literature on the theme of Partition and, more recently, on later memories, the Bengali or Punjabi experience, is highlighted; Papiya's work calls for foregrounding the missing link involving Biharis, both in the contiguous Bengal and in the inhospitable terrain of Sindh (though Sindhi nationalists might be confused by the expression 'inhospitable' with their celebratory claims of 5,000 years of continuous habitation since the time of Mohanjo Daro).

Papiya's work on Bihari Muslims was organized around three major book projects: (1) Pakistan movement in Bihar in the 1940s; (2) Partition and the Making of Bihari Muslim Diaspora in the latter half of the twentieth century; and (3) Dalit and backward Muslim contestation of the two-nation theory in the 1930s and 1940s, linking it to non-Ashraf assertions in contemporary Bihar.

Of these, the second project was completed in the form of a fascinating piece of work, *Partition and the South Asian Diaspora: Extending the Subcontinent* (New Delhi: Routledge, 2007). Unfortunately, the two other projects remained unfinished, but a collection of ten of her essays, previously published in national and international journals and as book-chapters, shows tremendous promise of what was about to come in the near future. The collection of her articles, *Community and Nation: Essays on Identity and Politics in Eastern India* (New Delhi: Oxford University Press, 2008) reveals the depth of her understanding of Bihar's Islamic tradition through the turbulent twentieth century and would appeal to wide readership, mainly those interested in Partition, refugee, diaspora, trans-national and peace studies with examples relating to a set of beleaguered Muslims, identified as Biharis.

In fact, the very idea of a homogeneous Muslim community is interrogated in Papiya's work through an analysis of the divergent, conflicting attitudes towards the two-nation theory and the Partition, involving leaders of the Jamiat-ul-Ulama-i-Hind (and of the Imarat Shariat, which serves as a parallel Shariat court), the Momin Conference of the Muslim weavers, the separatist Muslim League and the nationalist Muslim Congressmen. The position of the latter group was particularly difficult as they went around talking about *muttahida qaumiyat* (composite nationalism), even as leading Congressmen like Rajendra Prasad and Sri Krishna Sinha had strong links with the Hindu Mahasabha, scaring away Muslims of the minority province of Bihar to the fold of the Muslim League. Their exodus to Bengal and East Pakistan was marked by terrible violence back home.

As is by now common knowledge, 'Bihari' is a term of ridicule, even abuse, and may not necessarily indicate an ethnic or geographical identity, and would include Urdu-speaking Muslims from adjoining provinces like UP, though majority of them might actually have the province of Bihar as their place of origin. They may be especially noticed for their political assertiveness, even aggression, and visibility in public and a particular sense of pride, the source of which one is not very sure about. In terms of the introduction to the grand tradition of Islam and the perceived superiority of a Persianate-Urdu culture they might claim with some satisfaction an early exposure and sophistication when compared to the perceived cultural inferiority of rural Bengali Muslims, with whom they ran into trouble already in the 1940s.

A major part of Papiya's work traces the troubled history of Islam, involving Biharis and Bengalis in East Pakistan (and in Bangladesh since 1971), which, by implication, further aggravated communal relations in the Sindh province of Pakistan. Biharis, who identify themselves as Muhajirs or Stranded Pakistanis, are at the centre of a major concern in both Pakistan and Bangladesh, in between affecting India as well. Whereas all three modern nation states, which perhaps are still in the making, have not been able to adequately resolve the problem of how to tackle a huge population within the framework of citizenship and rights (to which I shall return subsequently), many enterprising individuals have been able to establish themselves, after several rounds of displacement and migration (Patna-Calcutta-Dhaka-Karachi), in such places as the Middle East, UK, US and Canada, creating a Bihari Muslim diaspora. Indeed, as some of Papiya's biographies also reveal, the best of Muslim self-expression in the West has some or the other connection with Bihar (often stretching up to Awadh and connecting with major locations like Allahabad and Lucknow).

Papiya's work, *Partition and the South Asian Diaspora*, closely follows the trajectories of several families and many individuals, who survived unprecedented carnage by sheer will power even as they were witness to many family-members and close relatives becoming victims of rape and murder sometimes in the name of religion (Islam and Hinduism) and sometimes language (Urdu, Bengali, Sindhi), major moments being 1946 riots in Bihar, Partition in 1947 and the creation of Bangladesh in 1971.

The well-structured monograph consists of four evenly-sized and densely footnoted chapters, besides a succinct introduction, which contextualizes and connects the Bihari experience with the larger discussion on Partition and its aftermath and the question of the settlement of refugees, and a short, futuristic conclusion on the unfolding scenario on the ethnic and religious fronts (the burning question of how to deal with the increasingly assertive minority population, especially in contexts where majority aspirations also remain unfulfilled), creating anxieties in large parts of contemporary South Asia today. Central to the theme of the four chapters – titled 'Negotiating Nations', 'Claiming Pakistan', 'Resisting Hindutva', and 'Redoing South Asia' – is a huge Muslim population which had supported the idea of Pakistan, but was rendered stateless as the very idea of the nation state based on religion, Islam, collapsed in less than twenty-five years of its foundation.

Papiya has knit together her account with varied sources: refugee statistics and reports, the archives of the diasporic repatriation activists, camp narratives, family histories, literature, interviews and email exchanges with the affected parties and interest groups.

In particular, the focus is on the miserable condition of over 35,000 families, comprising some 250,000 individuals, languishing in hutments of the size of 4 ft by 6 ft (and exceptionally in 6 by 8) in as many as sixty-six camps run by international agencies in many parts of Bangladesh. These refugees, who like to be called, Stranded Pakistanis, were amongst those Urdu-speaking Muslims, who had opposed the Mukti Bahini's liberation struggle, are languishing and waiting for their repatriation to Pakistan. Though many of the Bihari immigrants have been able to sneak away, before and after the creation of Bangladesh, to the territories of former West Pakistan and beyond, domestic political compulsions ensure that neither Pakistan nor Bangladesh are willing to provide citizenship rights to the stranded population which was at the centre of the horrendous idea of Partition involving massive displacement and migration, not to forget unprecedented violence both in 1946-7 and in 1971.

Whereas international law and norms and conventions for refugee settlements have been disregarded by Pakistan and Bangladesh with utter disdain, the Indian state's position in the matter is also intriguing. The unfinished business of the transfer of population caused by the hurried manner in which India and Pakistan were created and the latter dismembered with the emergence of Bangladesh has meant that even if the boundaries of these nation states are to be protected political conditions within these countries are compelling sections of populations, mainly minorities, to relocate themselves which often require crossing national boundaries illegally. Thus, in terms of responsibilities, the Indian government and sections of Hindu intelligentsia might welcome Hindu Bengali immigrants, even if illegal, grant them the status of 'refugees' and help them settle down within the Indian territories (In the language of Hindutva, it is the national duty of the Indian state and Hindus generally to ensure that the persecuted Hindu population of Pakistan and Bangladesh are protected by facilitating their settling down in India). However, if the illegal immigrants happen to be Muslims, whether Urdu-speaking or ethnic Bengali, they are identified as 'infiltrators' (from Hindutva point of view, Pakistan was created for and by these people and they have no right to live within Indian territories). Accordingly train-loads of 'Bangladeshis' are dumped at the border at regular intervals; they are a nowhere people left to fend for themselves, pressures from humanitarian advocacy groups notwithstanding.

Papiya has put together a heart-rending account of the struggles for survival, especially those who are identified as Partition's Biharis, tracing also the extraordinary career of those who defied all the hardships to win a life for themselves even if they might have lost their original home and close relatives. The fierce struggle between the Bihari outfit, Muhajir Qaumi Movement, and the Sindhi nationalist organization, Jiye Sindh Tahrik, for the control of Sindh and the larger struggle involving other ethnic communities such as Punjabis and Pukhtuns (as well as the entrenching of the Taliban and associated groups) have ensured that Pakistan as dreamt by Muslims in UP and Bihar in the 1940s was a weird concept. In many cases, the members of the extended family back in Bihar ensured that those who had migrated should not come back to claim their rights on their ancestral property by reporting to the police the overstaying of their relatives from the other sides of the borders. Elsewhere, in Western Pakistan, 'Bihari Roko Movements' have considerable support amongst other ethnic Muslim groups.

As shown by Papiya, in many cases, utter helplessness mark the Bihari reflection on what went wrong: they consider themselves as 'heroes' of the Pakistan movement, who were eventually reduced to the status of 'zeroes', as lesser-citizens and even non-citizens once Pakistan was created. In Urdu, they valued themselves as *hira*s (diamond) before Partition to become *kira*s (wretched insects) subsequently. Muslims have always celebrated their failures in Urdu poetry. Papiya has given several examples of the disappointments and hope expressed in Urdu verses. One of them quoted by Altaf Husain of the Muhajir Qaumi Movement hits at the crux of the problem:

Yeh waqt bhi dekha hai tarikh ke safhon ne |
Lamhon ne khata ki thi, sadiyon ne saza payi | |

[The annals of history have witnessed the phenomenon, That blunders committed in a short span of time unleash punishment for centuries.]

30

RELIGIOUS AND POLITICAL ENTANGLEMENTS IN MODERN INDIA

PROFESSORS MARTIN FUCHS and Vasudha Dalmia have edited an interesting collection of essays, *Religious Interactions in Modern India*. Vasudha Dalmia has also previously edited, with Munis Faruqui, a similar collection of essays on religious interactions in early modern India (sixteenth-eighteenth centuries), and has called it a 'sister volume'. Viewed together, this is an important project for understanding political resolution and management of religious traditions, for a relatively peaceful coexistence that explains the diversity and pluralism in Indian society, historically. Attempts to disturb the balance, equilibrium or consensus by fanning communal antagonism is a deeply flawed political strategy which fails in the long run, but not before considerably damaging the social fabric. Nonetheless, sanity prevails eventually. Bloodbath in the name of religion becomes a forgettable aberration. It cannot remain the order of the day, even in the most volatile of political situations. Therefore, a serious scholarly investment in religious literatures and traditions is a commendable exercise. It shows how religious communities continually refashion themselves, even though they keep harping on their traditional practices and markers of identity.

The volume under review comprises, besides an Introduction, 13 rigorously researched and detailed chapters, which are revised versions of a 2010 conference on 'Modernity, Diversity, and the Public Sphere: Negotiating Religious Identities in 18th-20th Century India', held at the Max Weber Centre of Advanced Cultural and Social Studies, University of Erfurt, Germany. These have been contributed by scholars working in broad areas of anthropology, history, literature, philosophy, religious studies and sociology. Together, they present a complex set of perspectives, which are possible through interdisciplinary approaches and conversations across disciplines. They, thus, offer a whole platter of erudite scholarship seriously reflecting on religious identities and interactions. This scholarship, as is increasingly the case with state of the art current research, is not only questioning the received wisdom on monolithic traditions such as Hindu, Muslim, Buddhist, Jain, and Sikh, but also showing amazing diversity and multiplicity within them. The relationships within as internal others, offshoots or sects and between larger communities such as Islamic and Hindu traditions are marked by a variety of experiences ranging from violent schism and discord and the felt need for peaceful coexistence. All these were guided by specific socio-political contexts, in this case of a violent British colonial regime, which tore asunder older practices and arrangements of communities on a subcontinental scale in the early modern era. Indeed, the lasting consequences of massive colonial transformations caused during the 'long nineteenth century' form the core of the focus of this large volume of essays.

It began with the mess in Bengal, which ultimately consumed its best mind in the early nineteenth century, Raja

Rammohun Roy, who was sort of convinced that the old early modern world had given way to the new colonial ideological perspective, in other words, colonial modernity. This was informed by forms of Christianity and called for reform within – in the process abandoning all things identified with Islamicate and precolonial, and, indeed, de-value them. Gita Dharampal-Frick and Milinda Benerjee locate the religious activism of Rammohun and William Wilberforce's emphasis on British imperial civilising mission in a 'nexus' between 'late precolonial' India and Britain. The discussion on the muddle of modernity debate would have certainly benefited from Partha Chatterjee's exposition of the clear distinction between early modern and colonial modern in India. Firmly established by 1830s, the colonial regime was determined to transform the colonized people forever, ensuring it through major interventions in social and cultural domains, besides looting and destroying the economy beyond redemption. As Barbara D. Metcalf shows in the next chapter, the princely state of Bhopal under the mid-nineteenth-century rule of Sikandar Begum, almost automatically embraced colonial modernity, for a matter of fact transition from the older form of Muslim statecraft to the new British model of a centralized administration, with the ruler styling herself as practicing a 'Protestant-style Islam', yet creating a fusion between tradition and modernity of sorts.

The presence of Jesuitical and Evangelical Christian missionaries and availability of print technology meant polemical debates were now possible on a bigger scale, quickly impacting a large population, as in the case of the study by Srilata Raman of a raging conflict in Shaiva

Siddhanta tradition in Tamil Nadu in the 1860s. Identified as 'a signature literary event of Tamil modernity', the reformists attempted something of a 'Protestantization' of Shaivism by insisting on returning to the canonical texts and thus standardizing the practices, which would adversely impact the lower caste and class with its revivalist agenda. The emphasis on need for correct practices and beliefs also affected the Jains in the nineteenth century, when the idea of a pan-India Jain community identity was developed, as shown by John E. Cort. The introduction of the British legal system and new communication technologies enabled the disputes to take new forms and called for determining what constituted a new Jain identity, with cases reaching colonial courts for mediation. One of the disputes involved Dayanand Saraswati, the founder of the Arya Samaj, who ran into what was by then an overarching Jain religious identity, Jainism. Dayanand clubbed Jainism with Buddhism and linked them with ancient Charvaka materialists. He also called for their eradication as, according to him, atheistic materialism was disastrous for Indian culture.

As Vasudha Dalmia illustrates in her chapter, the consolidation of Hindu religious traditions into what emerged as Hinduism, in late nineteenth and early twentieth century, involved downplaying pluralities and differences which could only be achieved through an imagined fear of a common and external foe, mainly Muslims. The attempts to build a particular kind of modern-day, narrow and exclusionist Hinduism involved not only ambiguities but also open disputes. This was sharply criticised by Mahatma Gandhi who worked with a broader, inclusive and conciliatory Hindu framework. As quoted by Dalmia, Gandhi put it in no uncertain terms:

> Wherever you find Arya Samajists, there is life and energy. But having the narrow outlook and a pugnacious habit, they either quarrel with people of other denominations or failing that, with one another.

The churning created by the British colonial regime not only produced larger Hindu and Muslim identities, but like Jains, other communities of people needed to consolidate themselves with sharper boundary-markers, often using older imaginaries. Anne Murphy draws insights from the Khalsa Darbar records of Sikh religious grants and control over sacred sites to explain that the Gurdwara Reform Act of 1925 recognized the Shiromani Gurdwara Prabandhak Committee as the single sovereign entity. This Committee was henceforth the custodian of not only Sikh religious property, but also of the new political community of the Sikhs whose life it governed alongside the management of *gurdwaras*. As is well known, this also led to a lot of exclusion. Another offshoot of medieval and early modern Bhakti movements, Dadupanthis also saw deep rifts between *sadhus* and householders on need for internal reforms under modern conditions. In her chapter, Monika Horstmann examines how sections of Dadupanthis were breaking away from older practices to invest in education. Connecting with Gandhian ideology, they sought to model themselves as Hindus in the service of a modern and Independent India. Dadupanthis were no longer militaristic *sadhus*. Their armed Naga wing was disbanded by 1938. Catherine Clementin-Ojha has delineated how the ideal of political *sannyasi*-hood was given a new lease of life by Swami Shraddhananda (1857-1926), through his late association with Gandhi and his speech at the 1919 session of the Indian National Congress. Thus, the idea of renunciation itself was secularized in the sense of providing moral authority on spiritual and ethical grounds for service to the people and liberating the nation.

Further, Kumkum Sangari shows Gandhi's logic of multiple belonging, formulation of ethical universalism, and emphasis on unity in diversity – of the kind Sufi and Bhakti sants preached and which included Muslims and untouchables – were so very relevant, but he eventually fell victim to Hindu exceptionalism. By contrast, the famous example of religious coexistence in the Punjabi princely state of Malerkotla, discussed by Anna Bigelow, offers hope. Despite prolonged religious disputes over disturbance in each other's prayers, the town escaped Partition-related violence and a large local Muslim population did not need to migrate to Pakistan. It was possible through a sagacious political regime ensuring that 'communal self-regulation and communication between religious communities' will protect the town's reputation as a crucible of peace.

In contexts where this conundrum of excessive entanglements of religion and politics is not resolved, the difficulties created by religious decrees have a direct bearing on the meanings of modern sovereignty and governance. In such situations, even voting in electoral politics is unduly influenced by notions of communal conscience on religious grounds, as explained by David Gilmartin in his chapter. Clearly, the aggressive separation of religion and politics, or church and state, which transformed early modern Europe in terms of clear distinctions between private and public, as delineated by Michel Foucault in his profound lecture on governmentality, did not happen in India. Rulers paid lip service to religion for legitimacy and kept pandering to pressures from religious sodality, with a mass of people ready to be unleashed as mobs. This is a problem the country is still facing with greater threat to the very idea of what the governments are expected to do, with dangers of anarchy looming large all around. Simple facts and truths are now being discarded in favour of fake news spread by social media and what is called, Whatsapp university of contemporary public domain.

With Islamic and Hindu traditions locked in a bitter struggle since at least the late nineteenth century, with accusations of forcible conversion and aggressive demands for *ghar-wapsi* almost shattering the public arena, does religious conversion as a political strategy actually help? The last two chapters in this volume address related concerns involving Dalit communities, untouchables, in the period of transition to post-colonial India. George Oommen analyses the struggles of the Pulayas in Kerala, who converted to Christianity through the Church Missionary Society's evangelization for some claim to their dignity as human beings and as liberation from the forms of slavery they had experienced in the past. This is a major concern in Kerala's Dalit history as also shown by P. Sanal Mohan's exhaustive research in the field. Conversion often does not help in mitigating the situation, and, therefore, such communities require political and governmental support as well. Besides internal othering by elitist upper-castes, conversion to Christianity is also a big issue for the Hindu right. Mercifully, Communist movement in Kerala provided some anchoring to the Pulaya Christians. They could also break away to establish a Church of their own, besides invoking social and historical memories in their attempt to shape a better future.

The other Dalit strategy was to embrace Buddhism for common good as explained by Martin Fuchs with reference to B.R. Ambedkar's critical theory of relationality – attacking the religious base of a society that supports caste-based 'graded inequality' and calling for a new universalism of solidarity. In Ambedkar's considered opinion, the teachings of Buddha, or *dhamma*, attaches the much needed sacrality to the principles of equality, liberty, fraternity and justice. These valued principles comprise moral universals laying ground for basic humaneness and sociability, which can help create a society with a respectful place for all; a society marked by solidarity and compassion – *maitri* and *karuna* – virtues otherwise lacking in general attitude towards the untouchables in particular. For Ambedkar, a good religion enabled protection of the weak and leading a worthy life.

The volume as a whole is a reminder of the terrible roles the mixing of religion and politics have played in the past couple of centuries. Despite claiming to be general do-gooders, religious groups have worked for hardening of community identities and pitted them all for a mess that is difficult to resolve. The saving grace is that after a certain level of violence they intervene for sanity through peace committees, comprising religious leaders, which assert that religion is against hatred and animosity. Despite obvious duplicity, there is some hope in this ambiguity. To conclude with Ambedkar's comment on the reality of a divinely-ordained hierarchy in society: 'Religion is a social force.... To ignore religion is to ignore a live wire.'

[Review of Martin Fuchs and Vasudha Dalmia, eds., *Religious Interactions in Modern India*, New Delhi: Oxford University Press, 2019. A shorter version has appeared in: *South Asian Studies*, 36(2), 2020, pp. 218-20.]

31

CONVERSION AND ISLAMIZATION IN INDIA

THE FOREIGNER tag notwithstanding, a large majority of Muslims in India appear to be local converts from politically marginal and socially deprived backgrounds, emerging as part of a variety of historical processes involving social and religious change over a millennium and covering vast swathes of territories across the subcontinent. The early ancestors of these Muslim communities from lowly caste and tribal groups might have been attracted to the somewhat liberating ideas of medieval Islam, hoping for alleviation of their condition – social uplift and immediate political benefits included. These were not rulers in medieval India by any stretch of imagination, despite occasional examples of exceptional rise of ambitious individuals of low origin converting to Islam and achieving high political positions. Thus, the assumption that conditions of Muslims in general have deteriorated since the colonial transitions in the nineteenth century into the current mess is faulty to an extent. Medieval India was not a golden age for all Muslims, but perhaps only for a small section of Muslim immigrants and for broadly Hindu collaborators, who were not required to embrace Islam to acquire important political positions.

A careful scrutiny of historical evidence regarding conversion and Islamization might help abandon some of the dubious conjectures and motivated conclusions. From this perspective, the defensive approach of secularist/pluralist historians of maintaining silence on this communally sensitive theme seems a flawed strategy. Even if communities and their demagogues might want to decide what is acceptable to them as history, it is important that a mature and historically informed society has a tolerant space for understanding the dynamic processes through which communities have come into being. Modern explanations of the making of Islam in the Indian subcontinent generally include immigration of Muslims from West and Central Asia, religion of the sword, egalitarianism of Islam as represented by Sufi brotherhoods unleashing landslide conversion, and the connected process of cultural accretion through a combination of factors – ecological, economic, social, religious, and, of course, political.

The attempts to look at long-term social and religious change, taking into account medieval sources on acceptance or rejection of Muslim customs and rituals, as well as comprehending medieval languages of politics and recognizing the lack of a centralized authority in Islam open up the possibility of a more complex understanding of the making of Muslim communities. The rulers sometimes invoked religion to justify their violent conquests, projecting them as *jihad* (holy-war). However, when it came to rule, just as they needed to dismount from the horses used for conquests, the narrow political ideals of orthodox Sunni Islam were also set aside. The *ulama*'s occasional pressure to forcibly convert non-Muslims was not taken seriously by the emperors, who paid lip service to Islam, but put emphasis on being just and benevolent, not discriminating between subject populations on the basis of religion.

Also, exclusionist political ideologies did not favour conversion, for new converts would expect equal rights and share in power. Complete decimation of non-Muslims was also not advocated, as power-relation could not be exercised in a vacuum. The supremacy and domination of Islam could only be established in counter-position to the inferiority and subjugation of others. Ziya-ud-Din Barani, the leading political theorist and historian of the Delhi Sultanate, summed up the ambiguity: the Sultans must uphold the principles of the Shariat (Islamic law), but the latter cannot be the basis of governance, nor should low-caste converts be given high political positions, monopolizing them for a small section of the entrenched elite. Thus, despite all the rhetoric of medieval Islamic violence and modern Hindu revenge, the fact remains that a vast Hindu population survived through the medieval centuries; it was not forced to migrate, slaughtered or converted to Islam.

Indeed, Muslim population at centres of so-called Islamic rule such as Delhi-Agra region remained minimal, with high concentration in regions at the margins of large Muslim empires. These communities have historically claimed that their ancestors embraced Islam at the hands of Muslim holy-men either directly or through the blessed presence of their shrines – a claim also made by Sufi fraternities even if early Sufi figures may not have worked with the explicit agenda of conversion. Sufis presented a humane face of Islam and played socially relevant roles, winning the hearts of the people through charitable endeavours and poetry of love in local languages, accommodating non-Islamic practices, and thus attracting a large number of followers without demanding formal conversion. In doing so, they heralded a process of Islamization, which was shaped by political developments, but not subject to any state coercion. This process is perhaps still continuing, even if the more Islamized and well-to-do Muslims might claim Perso-Arabic blood in their veins, risk being dubbed as outsiders, and charged with the natural reproduction hypothesis of *hum paanch aur hamare pachis*.

[Earlier published in the *Sunday Guardian*: http://www.sunday-guardian.com/analysis/conversion-was-not-forced.]

32

MUSIC IN ISLAM

ONE OF THE long-standing myths about Islam is that it is against music and related art forms such as singing and dancing. Occasional examples of moral policing by culturally-blind groups are touted as proofs of Islamic injunctions against music. In accepting such a misleading proposition, however, one of the finest chapters in the history of Muslim societies – of tremendous achievements of some outstanding cultural personalities across genres and repertoires – is subjected to a deliberate process of erasure. The saving grace is that a complete decimation of a cultural reality is not possible as Muslim societies have continued to produce a galaxy of poets, singers, instrumentalists and dancers, who have excelled as fine exponents of their respective fields of expertise. Importantly, some of the best artists have also been extremely devout and sincere Muslims.

Just a cursory look at the Indian art scene is enough to discard the misconception of Islam being opposed to music. The Bharat-Ratna Bismillah Khan spent a lifetime dedicated to his practice and performance of *shehnai*; the rest of his time was spent in prayers. Thus, *reyaz* and *namaz* remained the cardinal principles of his life, and there was nothing contradictory about his love for music and devotion to God.

As if Bismillah Khan was not enough, *dhrupad*, a form of music devoted to clearly identifiable Hindu deities, would be so much poorer without the remarkable contributions – almost on the verge of a healthy monopoly – of the Dagar brothers. Such has been the tradition of respect commanded by this and a host of other Muslim *gharana*s of music that even the most politically naïve *mufti* would not dare issue a provocative *fatwa*.

The history of growth and development of Hindustani classical music goes back seven centuries to the time of Amir Khusrau. One of the closest disciples of Chishti Sufi Hazrat Nizamuddin Auliya, the multi-faceted personality of Khusrau was able to receive patronage of a series of aesthetically suave Muslim Sultans of Delhi. Khusrau is not only reported to have developed various kinds of *raga*s, *khayal*s, and *tarana*s, but is also said to have invented or improvised a number of musical instruments, *mazamir* or *saaz* such as *sitar*, *sarod*, etc., which are central to classical musical performance. Even if Hazrat Nizam-ud-Din and other Sufi masters might have discouraged the use of instruments, his contemporary and later *qawwal*s would need a variety of instruments as accompaniments for their singing of songs of love and pain. And, despite restrictions put by the patriarchs, female *qawwal*s and singers have also succeeded in carving out a niche for themselves; imagine *ghazal* without Begum Akhtar, or *qawwali* without Abida Parveen today.

Music is not only central to devotional expression of love for God, Urdu/Hindi songs of Bollywood films have also been catering to the tastes of a variety of connoisseur. One does not need to dig into the dusty archive of a lost past to illustrate that some of the finest lyricists, singers, and composers associated with the Bombay film industry have come from Muslim cultural backgrounds. Such embarrassing characteristics are now being attributed to Islam and Muslims that it might appear a bit odd, for some, to realize that the Sahir Ludhianwis, Mohammad Rafis, Naushads and AR Rahmans carry Muslim names and there is nothing wrong in that. Like music, films are something that self-styled guardians have condemned as un-Islamic and unacceptable, yet a large number of Muslims are watching all the block-busters – first day, first show on the holy-day of Friday – being delivered by Salman Khan and other *badshahs* and Khan Bhais of cinema.

The theologians, on their part, could not have called for banning poetry altogether; the holy Quran is, after all, a versified text that continues to enchant billions of people. The regular call for prayers (*azan*) also requires people with a fine voice quality; it is not a mere case of rhetorical shouting from the roof-top or through a blaring loudspeaker. Prophet Muhammad himself was highly appreciative of the resonant voice of a manumitted Black slave and early companion, Bilal, known as the first *muezzin* (caller) for prayer in the mosque. The theologically recommended form of poetry also included unconditional submission to the will of God (*hamd*), loving devotion for the Prophet (*na'at*), and occasionally a subtle opening up of the longings of heart (*ghazal*) – expressing love (*ishq*) for the eternal divine (*haqiqi*) and never for a perishable this-worldly object of love (*majazi*). These forms – *hamd*, *na'at* and *ghazal* – are supposed to be recited, not sung, though in a melodious voice and conforming to *sur*. However, in medieval Islam also, the theologians could not check poetical forms such as the exaggerated phraseology of celebration of achievements of rulers (*qasida*), provocative outpourings of criticism in satires (*hajv*), and even sexy double-entendres (*iham-goi*), not to forget compositions inspired by the beauty of young boys as homo-erotic objects of love (*imrad-prasti*: not so much consensual homo-sexual love, but as a matter of fact *launda-bazi* (pederasty).

So, it boils down to which forms are acceptable and which not, aesthetically sophisticated genre vs those catering to popular taste, or classical/pop, good music/bad music. Within musicology also, the purists will argue for restrictions in language and elevation of forms, which can perhaps only be maintained for a small section of the cultivated audience with a *zauq* for refined expressions. For the little pleasures of the multitude, 'vulgar' forms are something which cannot be banished altogether for fear of being burnt in hell – real or imagined. Thus, standards of poetry and music are continuously set and re-set, according to the requirements of the time and place. For Hazrat Nizam-ud-Din, a connoisseur of music of the finest quality, it was irrational to issue a *farman* banning music altogether. For him and his fellow-travellers on the mystic path (*tariqat*), the standard of music and performance was important, including the content of what was being sung, accomplished singers, fine company of listeners, as well as a pleasant time and comfortable location.

In Sufi traditions, the *qawwal*'s touching utterances, both content and voice, should be sufficient to create ecstasy (*haal*) in a sincere aficionado, who might be allowed to gracefully rise and dance, whereas the fake enthusiasts could be easily identified for their drug-induced shrieks and hurried tearing of clothes, etc. Also, if compositions in Arabic and Persian were no longer helping raise over-powering emotions (*wajd* and *surur*), there was nothing wrong in listening to poetry in Punjabi, Awadhi, or Bengali. Further, for some occasions and those interested, *bhangras*, are not something to be condemned and banned; nor could anyone stop Wajid Ali Shah and his troupe from evolving, in the nineteenth century, the elegant dance form of Kathak, knowingly deploying legends and stories related to Hindu gods and goddesses.

Earlier, the seventeenth-century Mughal emperor Aurangzeb was rumoured to have banned music and, therefore, the aggrieved musicians took out a burial procession to bury music with all its trappings. Musicologists are now telling us that some of the finest theoretical texts on Hindustani classical music were not only written under Aurangzeb, but some were also dedicated to him. The emperor himself is reported to be an accomplished *veena* player. In conclusion, therefore, innocent children might still be encouraged to pray to God: *lab pe aati hai dua ban ke tamanna meri…meray allah burayi se bachaana mujhko*; even as the law-enforcing policemen can also enjoy the unruly public *mujra*: *mayen tow aayi hun UP-Bihar lootne*! As the foremost Sufi poet, Maulana Jalaluddin Rumi succinctly put it: only a donkey will have no taste for poetry and music. Others argued: even a donkey has a sense of music.

[Previously published in *Citizen Online*: https://www.thecitizen.in/index.php/en/NewsDetail/index/4/935/Music-is-The-Food-of-Love-in-IslamPlay-on.]

33

WOMEN IN *DARGAHS*

ONE OF THE defining features of popular devotion in the Indian subcontinent is the welcome presence of women at Sufi shrines. Therefore, it is so unfortunate and disturbing to hear of the attempt by some vested interests to ban the entry of women at Haji Ali Dargah in Mumbai. It is one of those irrationalities of our time that we are confronted with almost on a daily basis. There was a time, in the first centuries of Islam – for a millennium indeed – Muslims were setting standards of excellence in almost all fields of life, and now not a day passes without some self-declared custodians of Islam coming up with wicked and irrational ideas shaped by their regressive minds – bringing so much disrepute to a religious tradition, which was so liberating to start with.

If that thing called soul does exist, the Prophet of Islam, who must have been one of the finest figures of his time and a role model for Muslims for all time to come, must be turning in his grave. What is wrong with the communities of people claiming to be his true followers? As lovers of God and followers of the righteous path shown by the Prophet, Sufis and other Muslim holy-men would never discriminate against women in the manner in which the current guardians of Islam seek to bar them even from such spaces as a *dargah*

– a sacred space where they have historically been allowed to have a corner of their own as a sanctuary of relief from the oppressions of a patriarchal order that wants to subjugate them as toys or trophies as well as reproductive machines, mainly for a feudal society's fancy for male children.

For long, in large parts of the subcontinent, women have not been allowed to enter a locality mosque nor let in a graveyard till they are alive, and now some self-declared reformists want to block their entry into Sufi *dargah*s also on the ludicrous ground of patriarchal belief in women being impure for certain days in a month. Such occasions remind one of the historical memories of a galaxy of such fine souls in medieval Islam as redoubtable Rabiya of Basra, of the venerable Fatima Sam of Delhi, and of the miracle-working saint Bibi Kamalo in Bihar; these saintly women are known in history and popular traditions for their defiance of all the restrictions of the persecuting society of their times to work and fight for sanity and justice for all.

In the irrational times we inhabit, mobs are unleashed by extra-state actors for their little political benefits, those representing the state try to absolve themselves of any responsibility – as in the Haji Ali case in which the state does not want to be a party in the court, ink-throwing, lynching beef-eating suspects, and a host of other violations – political propagandists speak for history, and rumours and false reports are peddled as truth. These are signs of a society and its polity on an irreversible path of decline, at least in terms of the need for replacement of those in power with fresh ideas and energies to set things right.

For those who care, insights from history are tantalizing, and we are indeed heading into a forbidding time for a while.

All time great Muslim historian and proto-Sociologist, Ibn Khaldun (1332-1406), who looked at the history of rise and decline of the state from the perspective of what he called the science of human society, now identified as the Social Sciences, has said that it is not difficult to understand the unpredictability or fickleness of the human mind in certain social and political context: 'Traits of character are the natural result of the peculiar situation in which they are found.' So, for those in power, it is important to control the situation. Medieval theorists have also recommended the use of a heavy hand, especially when the violent mob is unleashed for creating anarchic situation. They had warned: a thousand years of dictatorship is better than one day of violence on the streets of the city, in a village or an island for that matter.

Our modern Social Scientists are also a product of the peculiar situation in which they are formed, few break-free from or rise above the filth of the socio-political reality, and that is why they do not command much respect. Indeed, few historians have been able to maintain what is referred to as historical distance and free themselves from biases for them to be recognized as a credible voice, and thus even illiterate followers of political groups as well as lonely fanatics on social media easily dismiss them as partisan, often using violent invectives.

Even if other cases are to be dismissed as occasional aberrations, what is a society worth if half of its population is scared away from a life in public, kept veiled in *purdah* in the hidden corners of their little dwellings and even possibly sought to be disenfranchized on the whims and fancies of a few clogged minds? And, all along, my thought goes to what Haji Ali himself would have thought about this madness around his sanctuary of peace. Are lovers going to be doomed and women deprived of whatever solace they would get from visiting the shrine?

[Previously published in the *Economic and Political Weekly*, 6 November 2015.]

34

THE STATUS OF DOGS IN ISLAM

GOING BY TRADITIONAL Islamic literature, opinions about dogs in Muslim societies were actually not as bad, both scripturally and historically, as is the general perception in modern times. Several Quranic verses refer to canines not only not as ritually unclean or unlawful, but also highlight many of their virtues including their universally recognized loyalty, besides their value in hunting and for protection of life and property. The Quran also includes the legendary story of the venerable Companions of the Cave, a maximum of seven saintly young men hiding and sleeping in a cave for many years to protect themselves from persecution. The Quranic version of the biblical tale also counts a dog, later named Qitmir, as an additional companion who protected others and slept with his forelegs stretched at the entrance of the cave.

Later traditions privileged cats over dogs, perhaps keeping in view the report of Prophet Muhammad's kindness towards his cat, called Muizza. The Prophet, however, recommended compassion towards all animals, including dogs, with a moving *hadis* of his posting a guard to ensure that a female dog and her newborn pups were not disturbed by his army, marching to conquer Mecca in 630 CE. Also, some middle-eastern tribes would not hesitate to call themselves Kalbi or Sagvand (that is, related to dogs: Arabic *Kalb*; Persian *Sag*). Indeed, one of the most handsome companions of the Prophet, who reportedly carried his message to the Roman emperor Heraclius (610–41 CE), was named, Dahiya Kalbi. Pious Muslims in subsequent generations have displayed, as a matter of pride, their complete deference and loyalty to the cause of Islam, prefixing their names as Kalb.

In medieval Sufi literature, a poignant anecdote on respect and love for dogs is related to Rabiya Basri, a first generation female Sufi par excellence, widely known for her public declaration of her mad love for God. Her aggressive condemnation of worship of Allah either for attractions of heaven or fear of hell, rather than unconditional love for Him, as well as violating conventional patriarchal norms meant, for the orthodox, she was destined to go to hell. However, after her death, she was seen in dreams of people who were still devoted to her and who asked her as to what treatment was meted out to her by God. She was reported to have said that all her idiosyncrasies or sins were forgiven because she used to feed a dog every night.

Medieval Indian Muslim holymen are also known to have kept dogs as companions and sometimes their tales became part of social satires. A fifteenth-century peripatetic Sufi, Sheikh Ahmad Abdul Haqq, had a female dog as pet during his stay in Rudauli/Awadh. The Sheikh invited the notables of the place for a feast to celebrate the birth of her pups. Next day, when a local Sufi, Sheikh Jamal Gujari, complained on not being invited, Sheikh Ahmad Abdul Haqq responded that only the dogs of the town were called for the feast held by his she-dog. The Sheikh added that, according to a tradition of the Prophet, the world was like a carcass and its seekers were dogs. He further said that he found Jamal Gujari as the only Muslim human being during his long journey from Sindh to Bengal and, therefore, he was not counted amongst the dogs invited for the party. Dog-lovers may find such anecdotes demeaning to their pets.

Islamic juristical positions bring out further ambiguities, with different schools maintaining different positions on levels of impurities or recognized values of dogs. For some, dog's hair is impure, so just touching it can be a cause of pollution; for others, touching or caressing a dog is not so much a matter of concern, but its saliva is *haram* and, thus, a source of ritual impurity. Yet, there is something of a consensus that a dog, domesticated or otherwise, was superior to a dim-witted donkey and loathsome pig, inferior to the multipurpose camel, and, despite fear of rabies, better than dangerous wolves and beasts.

In conclusion, Islam respects and enjoins protection of all beings – stones, trees, animals, humans, and generally the whole natural environment. An authoritative tradition of the Prophet puts it: if you are going to plant a sapling and suddenly hear that *qayamat* has been declared and the Day of Judgement has come, you should flee only after properly planting it. These sensitivities and distinctions are completely marginalized in contemporary discourses on Islam, which are obsessed with violent language of politics and where fragile sentiments are easily hurt.

[Previously published in *Citizen Online*: https://www.thecitizen.in/index.php/en/NewsDetail/index/9/285/Who-Says-Dogs-Have-no-Place-in-Islam-Canine-Qitmir-Debunks-This-Canard.]

35

COLOURS OF LOVE AND HATE IN TRADITIONS AND HISTORY

GREEN IS THE colour of love in ancient Hindu traditions, which medieval Sufis picked up to express their own love for God before it was passed on to or appropriated by various strands of modern Islam emerging from the Indian subcontinent since the early decades of the twentieth century. Much as Saudi Arabia, Iraq or Syria monopolize the limelight for matters Islamic, the crucial Indian connections to international Islamic movements – political and cultural practices – are often ignored. One such interesting link is the adoption from India of green as the predominant colour in Islamic societies in modern times. There has been a reverse flow from India of many things Islamic, which even the most experienced of the Islamologists in the West have not discerned and appreciated.

Drawing here from my ongoing research on colour symbolism in Islam and how modern politics often completely transforms and abuses older concepts and meanings embedded in them, green was the colour of sublime expression of love and attractions in ancient India's cultural traditions. Of all the principle emotions (*rasa*), Shringara is recognized as the finest, while others like Rudra (furious) and Bhayanaka (horrendous) will be identified as abhorring or repulsive. Each of these *rasa*s, nearly 11 of them, has a colour and a presiding deity associated with it. Shringara is celebrated in green with Vishnu as the deity, whereas the colours of terror and violence are red and black, with their own presiding deities prone to violence of the ultimate kind.

The association of green with Shringara Rasa and Lord Vishnu provides an important clue to its later association with Islam. It leads one to think of the possibility of understanding the connection between the association of the colour green with Islam in modern times and its meaning in ancient Indian performing arts and stagecraft, including dance and music. Thus, as one of the most prominent colours deployed in the context of love, marriage and prosperity in ancient Indian traditions, green was possibly adapted by medieval Indian Sufis to express their own love for God. Sufis devoted their whole life desiring union with their beloved God and their death anniversaries, *'urs*, literally marriage, are celebrated with much fanfare. The Sufis went around flaunting their love wearing turbans and, often, even upper garments of green colour, or by just throwing a green scarf over their shoulders, even though the most recommended colour for the Sufis' robe was blue – a colour associated with asceticism. Some sprinkling of saffron was also appropriated from Hindu mystics even by mainstream Sufis, often in skull-caps, though the more 'liberated' Muslim mystics did not hesitate wearing saffron clothes, asserting their own devotion to God in a 'competitive spirituality' of medieval *bhakti* kind. Counterfactually, how interesting it would be if Vaishnava *bhakti* or other strands of devotional movements would express themselves in green, instead of saffron!

Just as saffron is now identified with various shades of Hindutva politics, the colour green has been appropriated from Sufi groups into modern political Islam. Despite being heirs to a tradition of religiosity which throve on shared and dialogic practices, modern Sufi masters have often sided with separatist Muslim groups, as in the case of the overwhelming support of Sufi *pirs* in colonial Punjab for the Muslim League's demand for Pakistan. The flags they carried were splashed with various shades of green, in the process completely transforming the older Indic connotations of the colour; of love as in the Sringara Rasa or of fertility and prosperity as in the *varna* system, or the north-centric Vastu association of a cool green having calming effects. In course of time, the colour green was heavily used by Muslims not only in the subcontinent, but also in other parts of the world. Often, this has been at the cost of white, which is the colour of piety in Islam, though Saudi-inspired modern mosque buildings do emphasize the symbolism of white for Muslim religiosity of the fundamentalist kind.

Prior to the nineteenth century, the colour green is almost absent from all major mosques, tombs, gates, forts, palaces, and many other elegant structures. There is not even a single façade of green in the historic buildings of the Qutb Minar complex in Delhi. Imagine a smudged green Qutb Minar, or the Taj Mahal in polluted green; they would be eye-sores. Neither the Jama Masjid of Delhi of the thirteenth and fourteenth centuries (subsequently known as Qubbatul/Quwwatul Islam mosque, located in the Qutb complex) nor the Jama Masjid, built by Shah Jahan in Delhi, display the kind of green minarets and domes one comes across in Muslim localities in contemporary times.

The Quranic inscriptions, floral designs, and other forms of artistic expression shine in bright gold and attractive sprinklings of blue in most medieval monuments. Often, just simple engravings on plain marble would do. Not to forget, many religious decrees (*fatwas*) were issued against Muslim rulers wearing silk in golden or yellow colours. If the rulers had listened to the guardians of Sunni Islamic traditions, they would have to give an austere image of themselves by turning out in white robes in coarse cotton; nothing could be more farcical, given the rulers' self-expression of grandeur and magnificence channelled through various art forms, which were gracefully deployed for making statements of awe-inspiring power and resources they commanded. In this context, Mughal emperor Shah Jahan's vibrant style statements can be contrasted with his son Aurangzeb's politically calculated pretensions to piety and austerity.

Further, the major medieval forts, built or appropriated and maintained by Muslim monarchs – Qila Rai Pithaura, Purana Qila and Red Fort to name three well-known sites in Delhi – were made of red sandstone and other locally available construction material. The stylish finishing on these buildings will have the trappings of various colours other than green. Three colours, which actually attract attention, not only in medieval buildings, but also in vast repositories of extant paintings are the generous use of red, gold and blue. This is not only true of art and architecture in medieval India, but also for Central Asia, Iran and the Arab World through the middle-ages. Medieval Islamic monuments in major cities like Isfahan, Istanbul, Baghdad or Jerusalem represent a colourful and gorgeous world of Islamic architecture and not a monotony of green. So is the case with the refined Islamic 'artifacts' – including thrones and pulpits – now located in many international collections. Despite enduring violence involved in their re-locations, whether as gift items or as objects of loot, their polished designs glitter in gold, crimson, blue and several other pleasing combination of colours. Some of the most fascinating of Mughal miniature paintings reveal the predominant use of the combination of red, gold, yellow, white and blue. Only rarely a green-robed figure might be noticed in the miniatures and the person presented would, in all likelihood, be a mystic or religious figure devoted to God.

In modern times, in Muslim public buildings in India and abroad, one can find a preponderance of green, bordering on a bizarre kind of obsession if not fanaticism, irritating the aesthetically inclined. This, as mentioned earlier, could be of ancient Indian origin; just check out the *Natyashastra* or even the Vastu-expert nearby, someone who is not yet saffronized in the modern sense. Still with the rampant association of green with Muslims in recent times, Hindus – of whatever caste, creed or denomination they might be – would prefer, even for occasions such as marriage, a colour other than green, though in several communities and in various regions Hindu brides do wear green saris in some parts of the country. Yet, even as a red sari might be generally considered more auspicious in Hindu weddings now, the green glass bangles traditionally symbolize the prospects of marital bliss.

Muslim women appearing in public in their black *burqa*s might be an eye-sore for some, but it is mainly to ward off any ogling, if not the evil eye, though some are increasingly coming out in designer veils, both as fashion statement and new assertions of Islamic identity. Incidentally, black is the colour of mourning in Islam with the additional intention of revenge for any wrong-doing. Not connected to either of the symbolism, black has been the colour of the cloth used to cover the Ka'ba, a structure central to Islam with long pre-Islamic antecedents appropriated after a violent struggle. Mercifully, no one is complaining about the Muslim adoption of green for their religious and political expressions of various shades, though violence being perpetrated in the name of Islam, or against it, is a matter of serious concern.

As we are dealing with a sensitive matter and most issues tend to become sensitive in these days of intolerance, one may as well add that Muslims might like to believe that the colour green has been a part of Islam from the time of Prophet Muhammad who had a green flag in his army and later his tomb at Medina was also painted in green, but it was probably an innovation introduced by the Ottoman Sultans as the holy cities of Mecca and Medina were controlled by them in the early modern era. It is unlikely that the tribal Arab Sheikhs would paint the tomb green on their own. For different reasons perhaps, white robes for men in the desert must have been the preferred choice, as has been for the holy warriors and for our modern-day politicians – expressed in a fine Urdu word with some tinge of sarcasm, *safed-posh*. Further, if we are to accept early association of green as historically valid, the near absence of green in medieval Islamic iconography, except in representations of Sufis' turban or scarf, becomes inexplicable. In fact, the Prophet himself wore clothes of different colours, his banners were black when he fought against the infidels and he recommended praying in white garments; in peace-time, the black cloth used for the banner could double up as the turban.

We know that modern communal politics is often expressed in green or saffron. Despite polarization on religious lines, many people would like to go for a third option, which may not necessarily be red for now – politically or aesthetically – unfortunately. And, when one looks around at contemporary Islamic art and architecture, one is left thinking about the fate of shades of blue and turquoise, a predominant colour in medieval times which is conspicuously absent now. It could be that blue had a negative connotation, associated with blue eyes and their evil was warded off by putting blue as a decorative element just like the wearing of blue beads is supposed to repel the same. Significantly, the preferred colour for Sufis' robes in medieval times was blue, but in the Indian environment they also got enchanted by green.

Nothing is impossible in politics; in this case a sublime language of love has been transformed almost as a symbol of Muslim political identity. One wonders how the father of Indian theatrical art forms, Bharata Muni would have responded to modern-day political theatrics; for instance, can even the most accomplished of the politicians strike a reasonable balance between saffron and green? As the Quran would indicate, God, as a dyer (*rangrez*), could dye everything in his own colour of radiant light, which, He can splash on his sincere devotees such as Sufis and other divines. Splattered by God's colouring, colour distinctions disappear for the Sufis enabling them to rise above distinctions of caste or creed.

Politically, our apprehension is Delhi's Red Fort can be easily saffronized; and the Taj built by Shahjahan in white, and not green, can be vandalized and blackened by people who kill in the name of religion – people with no understanding of the cultural sophistication of their own ancient past.

[A previous versions of this work-in-progress was published in the *Economic and Political Weekly*, 16 January 2016.]

36

MIRZA GHALIB AND THE TRAGEDY OF 1857

THE LAST MUGHAL poet of Delhi, Mirza Asadullah Khan Ghalib (1797-1869), has presented a miserable account of his own plight during the revolt of 1857 in his heart wrenching autobiographical diary-like text, deceptively titled *Dastanbu*, meaning pleasant fragrance of my hands. Mirza Ghalib had to face immense difficulties during those fifteen months of trials and tribulations, between 11 May 1857 to 30 July 1858. This was especially so because his family pension from the British government was discontinued immediately after the outbreak of the revolt. The struggle for renewal of this pension remained an enduring story of Ghalib's life thereafter.

The revolt of the Indian soldiers and the attack on the British and the heinous actions by the latter in revenge badly affected the sixty-something Mirza Ghalib. The devastation at home and outside and the dreaded havoc caused all around are evident on every page of *Dastanbu*. The British revenge against the rebellion fell especially on Muslims. Ghalib writes that although his house was not directly looted by British soldiers, he had lost all his valuables and was also picked up for interrogation. Meanwhile, the pension regularly received from the British was stopped, as he was known for his association with the Mughal court.

Ghalib has himself provided a valuable historical perspective by throwing light on his life and work in *Dastanbu*. He says that the year 1857 coincided with the sixty-second year of his life of which nearly fifty years were spent on a poetic journey, of *sher-o-shayri*. He was just five when his father Abdullah Beg Bahadur had passed away. His uncle Nasrullah Beg Khan Bahadur brought him up like a son, but he also died when Ghalib was only nine years old.

Commanding 400 soldiers, Ghalib's uncle was in the service of British general Lord Lake, who had ensured two *pargana*s near Agra as his *jagir*. After his death, the British government withdrew both the *pargana*s. Instead, a monthly stipend was fixed for Ghalib and his younger brother, Mirza Yusuf, who incidentally died during the revolt after a prolonged mental disorder from which he suffered. The stipend was continuously received from the treasury of Delhi Collectorate till April 1857. Unfortunately, the door of that treasury was closed with the rebellion which broke out in May that year. This is despite the fact that Ghalib was sharply critical of the revolt and has written about it in this text.

The British were able to quickly recover in Delhi, but as Ghalib writes the situation was tense and rebel gangs were active for months in many towns and localities. He condemned them harshly, writing that many rebels were resorting to violence. According to him, they were unnecessarily fighting a lost battle. He feared that the stronger the struggle against the British, the more oppressive the latter would become in their retaliation. He, therefore, cursed the rebels, called the British just rulers and continuously reiterated his loyalty towards them. Meanwhile, he also continued to cultivate his personal relations and friendship with British officials, but the administration was not moved.

What was Ghalib's crime or fault? Did he commit any mistake to displease his British patrons? The answer is the British knew that Ghalib was not only a famous poet, but he was also a historian associated with the Mughal court. New political regimes seek to crush the historians associated with previous governments. They want to write history on the body of those they subjugate. Ghalib tried his best to get the British to accept him. The poet opposed the revolt of 1857 for this purpose. He also pleaded that the readers of his book should know that for all the magic of his pen when put to paper, he had depended for his livelihood on the British since his childhood, literally picking up grains from their dining table. However, none of this rhetoric helped. The finest Urdu poet of the eighteenth century, Mir Taqi Mir, would have anticipated the predicament:

Ulti ho gayin sab tadbiren kuchh na dawa ne kaam kiya|
Dekha is bimariye dil ne akhir kaam tamam kiya||

Historians can learn some lessons from Ghalib's tragedy, in terms of maintaining critical distance from political regimes, but then is it possible to steer clear of political power and remain neutral either? Can one also remain neutral in the wake of political violence all around? What may have put off the British with regard to Ghalib was that he was attempting to ride two horses simultaneously.

He has defended his position thus: seven-eight years back the Emperor called him to the court and asked him to write a new history of Timurid dynasty, for which an annual stipend of Rs. 600 was fixed. He had accepted this job and got busy with work. After a while, the Emperor's mentor or teacher in Urdu poetry (*ustad*), Zauq Dehlawi, passed away, and the responsibility of correcting and polishing the Emperor's poetry was also assigned to him.

Thus, Ghalib was not only writing an official history of the Mughals, but he was also honoured with the status of Bahadur Shah Zafar's master in Urdu *shayari.* During the revolt and after it was crushed, the precarious position of the Mughal emperor's close associates can be easily gauged. Many influential people were hanged, a large number of ordinary ones were also robbed and hacked even inside their homes. The Emperor himself was banished to Rangoon. Undoubtedly, the British showed their kindness to Ghalib by not harming him physically, though his pension was stopped, which could not be released again.

Referring to his job in the fort, Ghalib has pleaded that he had grown old and weak, and was accustomed to sit and rest away from the crowd, in a corner of his house. Also, because of increasing loss of hearing, deafness, he was unable to properly follow what people spoke at court and other public gatherings. He would, thus, force himself to visit the fort once or twice a week. If the emperor appeared in *diwan-i khaas*, he would remain in his presence, otherwise he would leave after sitting there for some time. During this period, whatever work was completed, he would carry with him or send through someone. This was the sum total of his work and connection with the court. For the British, this may have sounded like the usual story of Indian deception they were accustomed to hear from the people they had colonized.

Unfortunately for us, the history that Ghalib was writing is not extant now. Or, is it that it is available and since modern historians have not worked even on this aspect of Ghalib's career as a Mughal court historian that we do not know about this? A complete history of the Mughal rule in its last days by none other than Ghalib would have been such a literary masterpiece, which all historical classics are supposed to be. Sadly, this was not to be. Ghalib could sense the revolution of sorts taking place in the world around him, which was going to do away with the old world peace and comfort and destroy his life, which, he claimed, was free from any kind of evil.

The violence that broke out on 11 May 1857 shook the ramparts of the forts and walls in Delhi, with rebel soldiers going on a rampage, fatally attacking English officers wherever they were spotted. People like Ghalib who remained loyal to the British helplessly heard reports of violence by the rebels. Not long after, they also dreaded a more aggressive retaliation by the British when the latter set out to crush the revolt with a heavy hand. The way Ghalib has expressed his regret over British casualties, condemned the rebels and lamented his own helplessness, how good for Ghalib and others it would have been if the British had accepted their loyalty during the revolt and after.

The reports of events during those fifteen fraughtful months reveal that with the revolt being crushed, the elite sections of the old Muslim society were made to realize that the times had changed and it would no longer be possible for them to thrive on old world privileges. In particular, this story of Ghalib's tragedy is heart-wrenching. He kept crying:

Dile nadan tujhe hua kya hai
Akhir is dard ki dawa kya hai |

Ham hain mushtaq aur woh bezaar
Ya ilahi yah maajra kya hai||

Seen from Ghalib's point of view, it is a matter of regret that all his efforts to gain the trust of the British had failed. On the other hand, because of his opposition to the revolt of 1857, Indian nationalist historiography, of which there are several strands, has also deemed it necessary to steer clear of Ghalib's life and career. Just imagine: no credible historian of modern India, or specifically of 1857, thought it necessary to study Ghalib, certainly not his *Dastanbu*. This would have been a misfit in the massive celebration of 150 years of the 1857 revolt a decade ago. They spoke on everything except Ghalib's eye-witness account of the rebellion and its condemnation. Thankfully, scholars studying Urdu literature and its history have preserved Ghalib's name and identity, besides his gaining immense popularity in posterity, across regions beyond Urdu speaking areas.

On his own, grappling with all the problems, Ghalib stood firm on his iconoclastic assertions:

Hoga koyi aisa bhi ke 'ghalib' ko na jaane|
Shayar tow woh achha hai pe badnam bahot hai||

And:

Puchhte hain woh ke ghalib kaun hai|
Koyi batlao ke ham batlayen kya||

Thus, Ghalib immersed himself in his exquisite Urdu poetry, especially Ghazal, which is, in other words, a means to cultivate the heart to gracefully embrace failures in life. In addition, the poet also networked with a large number of people through his famous letters. A collection of his 341

Persian letters, addressed to as many as 84 people, throw lights on Ghalib's versatile personality, his sad helplessness and relentless attempts to overcome the difficulties. Happily, Ghalib also resorted to humour and laughed at his own tragedy and on other people's stupidities through his popular jokes. He would announce:

Maine mana ke kuchh nahin ghalib |
Muft haath aaye tow bura kya hai | |

CONCLUDING REMARKS: STRUGGLE FOR PEACE IN VIOLENT POLITICAL TIMES

THE FOREGOING PAGES were part of the attempt to highlight the importance of bringing history and the historian out of university libraries and classrooms, to the public domain. This is especially needed in the context of so much misinformation and misrepresentation. The search for peace in violent political times takes us back to Indian history for some insights from political conquests, political theory, governing principles and resolution of community relations. The pluralistic form of society is historically marked by ethnic and religious multiplicity, and respectful coexistence, with concerned scholars and thinkers speaking out for the rights of even those languishing at the bottom of a regressive social hierarchy and political marginalization.

The medieval and early modern period of Indian history witnessed broad and inclusive framework of political ideas, theories and practices adopted by Mughal emperors like Akbar. By contrast, rulers like Aurangzeb drew on narrow sectarian ideologies, especially invoking the name of Sunnite Islam for legitimizing some of the outrageous political aggrandizement. Violence was possible in the wake of conquests and empire-building, but medieval works on political theory advocated minimum use of force under all circumstances. To cite the well-known example, Abu'l Fazl's *Akbarnama* and *Ain-i Akbari* articulated Mughal political ideology on how to govern a vast subcontinental country with so much diversity, especially for resolving the question of religious assertions through emphasis on broad-based governing principles, conceptualized as peace with all. It was understood that political conquests might involve episodes of violence, but governing principles of the state had to be inclusive and just, offering space for all the heterogeneity to respectfully coexist.

The examples of what medieval rulers did can serve as useful insights. Considerable political sagacity was displayed in handling the people, traditions, customs, religions, languages and diverse ways of living which have survived till modern times. Caste-based social stratification was not disturbed and sections of assertive communities were continually incorporated in the political system. Traditional and customary practices were dealt with in such a manner that the communities concerned did not feel threatened. Linguistic and ethnic pluralism were intelligently handled, evoking strong faith in the protective umbrella of the state. With strong commitments to justice for all, rulers themselves acquired or were accorded divine-like characteristics, which also meant combining the contradictory qualities of enjoying unlimited power, yet displaying amazing magnanimity and forgiveness to those seeking protection.

Even though much violence, bloodshed and destruction were possible during the conquests, once the opponents were defeated in the battlefield, the former rivals were co-opted and allowed to work as subordinate or trusted allies. Emphasis on protecting human resources and talents was recommended in works of political theory and also seen in practice. Places of worship too were protected, with only ones caught in political struggles being targeted. Rulers who are reported to have demolished some places of worship also gave generous grants for maintenance of religious establishments of the same communities who were seemingly affected by aggressive vandalism. No wonder, some of the finest religious buildings have come down to us from medieval times.

Intersecting political and cultural domains, Sufi-*bhakti* complex also preached peaceful coexistence and tolerance of other people's religious beliefs and practices, which further explains the amazing diversity we have inherited. In this context, we need to take cognizance of cases of belligerent sectarianism, complex identity formation, questions of conversion, and occasional attempts to abuse political power in the name of religion. Unlike early modern Europe where the emperors had realised that since they had the resources to conquer and build an empire they had the power to control and govern also, medieval and early modern Indian rulers continued to seek religious legitimacy for political action, which meant state could not be properly secularized, nor was religion made a private or personal matter of individuals. As a result, the state continually abused religion for asserting its power, and in return religion threatened the governing principles of the state. This tricky relation between politics and religion always needed a sane, balanced and careful handling – ensuring governing principles were privileged over sectarian considerations.

Thus, we need to know specific cases of religious justification of violence during battles for conquests and state-building, examine political principles and frameworks (since the conquerors needed to come down from their horses and establish their rule), and understand continuous attempts at resolving religious and cultural tensions. This will help us move away from the usual binary: either celebrating or condemning political violence and bloodshed, or completely denying the cases of violence – emphasizing, instead, the struggle for peace as actual example of peaceful community relations. Violence cannot be the order of the day, which is the very reason why we need states and governments and yet those in the business of politics and power need to be regularly reminded of this important responsibility. History has for long taught us mass violence and genocide are to be banished for some sanity in society. Political madness of the violent kind can only be an aberration and not the norm.

Political domain entails activism, propaganda, ideology, history, theory as well as philosophy. At the bottom of the pit, engagement in third-rate politics takes the form of back of the lane stabbings and confrontations – where the boundary between crime and politics gets blurred. By contrast, in all civilized societies, scholars, writers, historians, political theorists and philosophers have always been at the top of the social and political order. Scholarly excellence demands that members of academic community should aspire for the highest of the intellectual plane – maintaining graceful distance and, accordingly, treated with dignity. In any civilizational history, scholars and intellectuals occupy a prominent position since without their contribution credible histories would not be possible – though some political propagandists could offer a tunneled vision of dominant political ideologies celebrating achievements of conquerors and rulers.

Certainly, in times of political instability, state and competent rulers are needed for ensuring political stability, managing community relations in societies with vast diversities, law and order, peace and tranquillity, enforcement of a progressive law with the idea of justice for all – as law cannot be discriminatory – and general economic well-being of people; what could be termed as development. There are moments when governments and states fail to deliver, when third-rate theologians are privileged over first-class intellectuals, for the former can legitimize political abuse of religion, whereas critical unbiased scholars would question violations of standard norms fearlessly. As historian and political theorist, Ziya-ud-Din Barani stated in the fourteenth century, historians and intellectuals should steer clear of any falsehood.

In India, we have thousands of years of civilizational achievements of excellence in different spheres of life – political, economic, social and cultural. They provide us with strength and confidence that divisive politics may push us towards the abyss at times but sanity eventually prevails; religious justification of violence takes a back seat to pragmatic governance and peace. The unity in diversity slogans such as *sarv-dharm sadbhav / mazhab nahin sikhata apas mein bayr rakhna* highlight the value of peaceful co-existence. Cultural separatism and domination is set aside in favour of shared traditions and history. Common customs and practices lead us forward. Tolerance of difference and state maintaining equitable distance from sparring religious communities have frequently found favour in our past. Whatever the provocation and no matter who is in power, violence on the streets is condemnable as it defies the logic of the existence of the state itself.

Great empires and states have shown that inclusive politics is always better as it unites people for peaceful co-existence; they have recognized diversity and value of pluralism and the prosperity these ideas generated. On the other hand, aggressive and extremist political position divides and excludes people, supports an unjust order and condones violence. Unleashing violent mobs on university campus, for instance, should certainly be an aberration and not the norm in any civilized society. Despite all the limitations and challenges – identity-politics, ideological struggles and fear of violence – the parameters of historical research have expanded and historians are arriving at some approximation of truth. Instead of insisting on an absolute truth, they are now recognizing the possibility of space for difference of opinion and multiplicity of interpretations and perspectives. In all these, the conventional commitment to the protocols of historical research, method and practice are upheld, especially with regard to the primacy of evidence, asking a whole new set of questions and offering reasonable arguments in fine narratives.

Some finest examples of this present research includes new histories of competitive religious practices, sophisticated political theories, questions of sovereignty, vibrant literary and historical traditions, fascinating visual cultures studied through art historical methods, consumption and trade, as well as outstanding issues of regional, caste, gender or linguistic identities. Nations and nationalists are important, but regions are asserting and their assertions are reflected in varied new regional histories. And thankfully, despite all the abuses heaped on it, some exhilarating research in recent years has established that medieval India too was not a dark age!

The enduring international image of India is of a peace-loving country with a long history celebrating the language of love and tolerance amongst its diverse population, comprising a variety of ethnic and linguistic communities, with rich traditions of political and intellectual achievements going back to the dawn of human civilization. The everlasting cry for the notion of brotherhood among Hindus, Muslims, Sikhs and Christians, at times, sounds clichéd, but it is always recognised as a socio-political ideal of unity in diversity. Religious appropriations and tensions apart, men of religion had long understood the need to control raw emotions of their followers, so that they behave responsibly, recognizing religious difference with some degree of civility and a complete no to violence. This is what the Chishtis taught us, as did Sant Kabir and Guru Nanak – religious preceptors, par excellence.

Further, texts on political theory and norms of governance have historically emphasized the need for a system disapproving discrimination in the name of religious difference, or hierarchies based on birth and power for that matter, with a sincere commitment for justice for all. The fourteenth-century Delhi Sultan, Muhammad bin Tughlaq may have had his own specific rationality, but the arbitrary and often violent manner in which he seemingly conducted the business of state led even his closest well-wishers and associates eventually to dump him, leaving such a forbidding image of his for posterity. And, as we have long understood, it is so easy to condemn or abandon someone like Aurangzeb for whatever irrational things he might have done.

Also, intellectual freedom and excellence in a variety of fields ranging from philosophical and other-worldly concerns to emotional and bodily practices – love and sex – cannot be suppressed forever. The society was certainly not so prudish and repressive in ancient times as it might appear from horrible dictates of village *khap-panchayats* today; and this should certainly not be the ideal of a modern state promising good governance.

In our more recent history, Gandhian politics epitomized the power of the weapon of truth and non-violence. The significance and effectiveness of this language of peaceful resistance in modern times have reinforced India's formidable image, internationally – not only in Central Asia, Iran, Africa and the Middle East, but also in the United States. The struggling people in Afghanistan, Palestine, and large parts of Africa have for long looked up to India to play an important role in helping resolve the problems facing them – problems not of their own making by any stretch of imagination.

The trigger-happy, frustrated, and hawkish sections amongst Indians might be getting desperate, but the policymakers and others in the business of government can only act in a sensible manner. For, it will be disastrous for India to abandon its historic role as a responsible nation, and there are enough safeguards and signals to ensure this will not be the case.

Meanwhile, some people will continue to suffer: desperate Rohingyas in Myanmar, wretched Biharis in Bangladesh, hapless Hindu and Sikh minorities at the hands of the Taliban in Pakistan and Afghanistan, with the states utterly failing in ensuring justice for these innocent people, the miserable Palestinians in their own motherland, and those at the receiving end of ISIS bloodbath in the name of Islam, for which there is absolutely no justification.

Majoritarianism anywhere is a dangerous thing. Minorities can have a space for themselves in a constitutional democracy and can survive temporary violence, but in regimes thriving in the name of religious or cultural nationalism there are moments when the perpetrators can get away with serious human rights violations with long-term consequences. None of the above kind of difficulties is possible on Indian soil, for those in power have to necessarily adhere to the principles of a firmly-grounded Indian state, which are above the narrow and partisan interests of political parties and vote-banks.

Thus, pragmatics of running a state requires a leader and polity that provide justice, some kind of reasonable state laws and policies, and welfare of the poor as well as space for critical intellectual pursuits. Temporary setbacks notwithstanding, the chequered history of India's civilizational achievements cannot be undone by narrowly-conceived political ideologies which can dominate only in short and dark patches.

GLOSSARY

Advaita	Non-dualism in Vedantic doctrine of Hindu tradition
Amalaka	Myrobalan fruit, crowning member of a Nagara temple
Arzal	Vile, ignoble, the vulgar
Asharama	Hermitage
Ashraf	Nobles, grandees, men of high birth
Avatara	Divine incarnation
Baba	spiritual figure
Bakhar	Marathi historical narrative
Bhakti	Complete devotion to God
Buranji	Assamese historical literature
Charit	Biographical narrative of a historical or legendary character
Dargah	Large Sufi shrine, tomb
Darshan	Seeing a saint or a holy image
Dhamma	Truth as set forth in Buddha's teaching
Dharma	Religious and moral duty in Hindu traditions
Dhrupad	A genre in Hindustani classical music
Faqir	Mendicant, dervish, poor
Farman	Royal order or command

Fatwa	A judicial decree pronounced by a Muslim *mufti*
Firqa	Sect, community
Fitna	Sedition, anarchy, calamity, discord
Ganja	intoxicant, cannabis
Ghazal	Poetry of love
Guru	Spiritual leader
Hajv	Satire or lampooning in poetic mode
Halal	Permissible, allowed in Islam
Hamd	Poetry in praise of God
Haram	Forbidden, unlawful in Islam
Hashish	Drug made of cannabis
Ishq	Love
Itihas	History
Jagir	Land assignment
Jalal	wrathful, mighty power
Jamal	Elegant, graceful
Jizya	Capitation tax, initially paid by Jews and Christians in an Islamic regime
Karamat	Miracle performed by Sufi saints
Kavya	Poetic compositions
Khalifa	Spiritual successor of a Sufi, caliph
Khayal	A form of Hindustani classical music, named after imagination or meditation
Khutba	Sermon, especially preached in the mosques on Fridays
Makara	Mythological, hybrid crocodile-like sea creature
Malechh	Dirty barbarian
Math	Monastery in Hindu traditions
Mazar	Grave
Mazhab	Religion, school of jurisprudence in Islamic traditions

Muezzin	The person who proclaims the calls for prayer in mosques
Mufti	Expounder of Muslim law, giver of *fatwa*
Muhtasib	Censor official
Murtadd	Apostate
Na'at	Poetry in praise of the Prophet of Islam
Namaz	Muslim form of worship
Nirgun	Devotion for a formless God
Panth	Community of the Sikhs
Pir	Sufi master
Qasida	An elegy, poetry of praise
Qawwali	Singing and playing musical instruments in Sufi traditions
Qayamat	Day of Judgment in Islam
Qazi	Judge
Rekhta	Mixed language, early Urdu
Sagun	Worship or devotion for God with form
Sanyasi	An ascetic or religious mendicant
Shariat	Islamic law
Silsila	Sufi order, or spiritual genealogy
Sufi	Muslim mystic
Sulh-i kul	Peace with all, perfect or absolute peace
Tarikh	History
Tariqat	Sufi path or practice
Tauhid	The concept of unity of God in Islam
Ulama	Muslim religious scholars (singular: *aalim*)
Urs	Death anniversary of Sufis
Vanshavali	Genealogical accounts
Wahdat-ul-wujud	Unity of existence

SELECT BIBLIOGRAPHY

Ahmad, Aziz, 1964, *Studies in Islamic Culture in Indian Environment,* Oxford: Clarendon Press.

A'in-i-Akbari of Abu'l Fazl, English translation by H.S. Jarrett, second edition, edited and annotated by Sir Jadunath Sarkar, vols. II-III, reprint, Delhi: Low Price Publications, 1997.

Akbarnama of Abu'l Fazl, English translation by H. Beveridge, vol. III, reprint, Delhi: Low Price Publications, 2007.

Alam, Muzaffar, 1986, *Crisis of Empire in Mughal North India: Awadh and the Punjab*, New Delhi: Oxford University Press.

———, 2004, *The languages of Political Islam in India, circa 1200-1800*, New Delhi: Permanent Black.

———, 2021, *The Mughals and the Sufis: Islam and Political Imagination in India, 1500-1750*, Ranikhet: Permanent Black.

Aquil, Raziuddin, 2007, *Sufism, Culture, and Politics: Afghans and Islam in Medieval North India*, New Delhi: Oxford University Press.

———, 2017a, *Lovers of God: Sufism and the Politics of Islam in Medieval India*, New Delhi: Manohar.

———, 2017b, *The Muslim Question: Understanding Islam and Indian History*, New Delhi: Penguin Random House.

———, 2020, *Days in the Life of a Sufi: 101 Enchanting Stories of Wisdom*, New Delhi: Pan Macmillan.

Aquil, Raziuddin and Partha Chatterjee, eds., 2008, *History in the Vernacular*, Ranikhet: Permanent Black.

Aquil, Raziuddin and David Curley, eds., 2016, *Literary and Religious Practices in Medieval and Early Modern India,* New Delhi: Manohar and London and New York: Routledge.

Aquil, Raziuddin and Tilottama Mukherjee, eds., 2020, *An Earthly Paradise: Trade, Politics and Culture in Early Modern Bengal*, New Delhi: Manohar and London and New York: Routledge.

Asar-us-Sanadid of Sir Syed Ahmad Khan, Delhi: Urdu Academy, 2000.

Asher, Catherine B. and Cynthia Talbot, 2006, *India Before Europe,* Cambridge: Cambridge University Press.

Asif, Manan Ahmed, 2020, *The Loss of Hindustan: The Invention of India*, Cambridge, Mass.: Harvard University Press.

Behl, Aditya, 2014, 'Emotion and Meaning in Mrigavat?: Strategies of Spiritual Signification in Hindavi Sufi Romances', in *After Timur Left: Culture and Circulation in Fifteenth-Century North India*, ed. Francesca Orsini and Samira Sheikh, New Delhi: Oxford University Press.

Bhargava, Rajeev, 2010, *The Promise of India's Secular Democracy,* New Delhi: Oxford University Press.

Bhattacharya, Neealdri, 2008, 'Predicaments of Secular Histories', *Public Culture*, 20(1): 57-73.

_____, 2018, *The Great Agrarian Conquest: The Colonial Reshaping of a Rural World*, Ranikhet: Permanent Black.

Bilgrami, Akeel, 2014, *Secularism, Identity, and Enchantment*, Ranikhet: Permanent Black.

Brown, Katherine B., 2007, 'Did Aurangzeb Ban Music?: Questions for the Historiography of his Reign', *Modern Asian Studies*, 41 (1): 77-120.

Busch, Allison, 2011, *Poetry of Kings: The Classical Hindi Literature of Mughal India*, New York: Oxford University Press.

Chakrabarty, Dipesh, 2015, *The Calling of History: Sir Jadunath Sarkar and His Empire ofTruth,* Ranikhet: Permanent Black.

Chatterjee, Kumkum, 2009, *The Cultures of History in Early Modern India: Persianization and Mughal Culture in Bengal*, New Delhi: Oxford University Press.

Chatterjee, Partha, 2020, *I am the People: Reflections on Popular Sovereignty Today*, Ranikhet: Permanent Black.

Chatterjee, Partha and Anjan Ghosh, eds., 2002, *History and the Present*, Delhi: Permanent Black.

Chaudhuri, Supriya, ed., 2022, *Religion and the City*, London and New York: Routledge.

Curley, David L., 2008, *Poetry and History: Bengali Mangal-Kabya and Social Change in Precolonial Bengal*, New Delhi: Chronicle Books.

Currie, P.M., 1989, *The Shrine and Cult of Muin al-Din Chishti of Ajmer*, New Delhi: Oxford University Press.

Dale, Stephen F., 2018, *Babur: Timurid Prince and Mughal Emperor, 1483-1530*, New Delhi: Cambridge University Press.

Dastanbu of Mirza Ghalib, Urdu translation from original Persian, New Delhi: Taraqqi Urdu Bureau, 2000.

De Bruijn, Thomas, 2012, *Ruby in the Dust: Poetry and History in Padmavat by the South Asian Sufi Poet Muhammad Jayasi*, Leiden: Leiden University Press.

de Certeau, Michel, 1988, *The Writing of History*, English translation by Tom Conley, New York: Columbia University Press.

Deshpande, Prachi, 2007, *Creative Pasts: Historical Memory and Identity in Western India, 1700-1960*, Ranikhet: Permanent Black.

Dhar, Parul Pandya, ed., 2021, *The Multivalence of an Epic: Retelling the Ramayana in South India and Southeast Asia*, Manipal: Manipal Universal Press.

Digby, Simon, 1983, 'Early Pilgrimages to the graves of Muinuddin Sijzi and other Indian Chishti Shaikhs', in *Islamic Society and*

Culture: Essays in Honour of Aziz Ahmad*, ed. M. Israel and N.K. Wagle, New Delhi: Manohar.

———, 1986, 'The Sufi Shaykh as a Source of Authority in Medieval India', *Purushartha*, 9: 55-77.

Drayton, Richard, 2011, 'Where Does the World Historian Write From?: Objectivity, Moral Conscience and the Past and Present of Imperialism', *Journal of Contemporary History*, 46: 671-85.

Eaton, Richard M., 1994, *The Rise of Islam and the Bengal Frontier*, New Delhi: Oxford University Press.

———, 2002, *Essays on Islam and Indian History*, New Delhi: Oxford University Press.

Eaton, Richard M. and Philip Wagoner, 2014, *Power, Memory, Architecture: Contested Sites on India's Deccan Plateau*, New Delhi: Oxford University Press.

Ernst, Carl W., 1992, *Eternal Garden: Mysticism, History and Politics at a South Asian Sufi Centre*, Albany: State University of New York Press.

———, 2016, *Refractions of Islam in India: Situating Sufism and Yoga*, New Delhi: Sage/Yoda Press.

———, 2017, *It's Not Just Academic! Essays on Sufism and Islamic Studies*, New Delhi: Sage/Yoda Press.

Ernst, Carl W. and Bruce B. Lawrence, 2002, *Sufi Martyrs of Love: The Chishti Order in South Asia and Beyond*, New York: Palgrave Macmillan.

Farooqi, Mehr Afshan, 2021, *Ghalib: A Wilderness at My Doorstep*, Gurgaon: Penguin Random House.

Faruqi, Ziya-ul-Hasan, 1996. *Fawa'id al-Fu'ad: Spiritual and Literary Discourses of Shaikh Nizamuddin Awliya/Originally Compiled by Amir Hasan 'Ala' Sijzi Dehlawi*, English translation with introduction and historical annotation, New Delhi: D.K. Printworld.

Faruqui, Munis D., 2014, 'Dara Shukoh, Vedanta, and Imperial Succession in Mughal India', in *Religious Interactions in Mughal*

India, ed. Munis D. Faruqui and Vasudha Dalmia, New Delhi: Oxford University Press.

Fletcher, Joseph F., 1995, 'Integrative History: Parallels and Interconnections in the Early Modern Period, 1500-1800', in *Studies on Chinese and Islamic Central Asia: Collected Articles of Joseph Fletcher*, ed. Beatrice F Manz, Aldershot: Variorum, pp. 1-35.

Foltz, Richard C., 2007, *Animals in Islamic Tradition and Muslim Cultures*, Oxford: Oneworld Publications.

Friedmann, Yohanan, 2003, 'Islamic Thought in Relation to the Indian Context', in *India's Islamic Traditions, 711-1750*, ed., Richard M. Eaton, Delhi: Oxford University Press, 50-63.

Fuchs, Martin and Vasudha Dalmia, eds., 2019, *Religious Interactions in Modern India*, New Delhi: Oxford University Press.

Gandhi, Supriya, 2019, *The Emperor Who Never Was: Dara Shukoh in Mughal India*, Cambridge Mass. and London: Harvard University Press.

Ghosh, Papiya, 2007, *Partition and the South Asian Diaspora: Extending the Subcontinent*, New Delhi: Routledge.

_____, 2008, *Community and Nation: Essays on Identity and Politics in Eastern India,* New Delhi: Oxford University Press.

Ginzburg, Carlo, 1991, 'Checking the Evidence: The Judge and the Historian', *Critical Inquiry*, 18(1): 79-92.

Green, Nile, 2006, *Indian Sufism since the Seventeenth Century: Saints, Books and Empires in the Muslim Deccan*, London: Routledge.

_____, 2012, *Making Space: Sufis and Settlers in Early Modern India*, New Delhi: Oxford University Press.

Habib, Mohammad, 1974 and 1981, *Politics and Society during the Early Medieval Period: Collected Works of Mohammad Habib,* vols. 1-2, ed. K.A. Nizami, New Delhi: People's Publishing House.

Haqq, M. Enamul, 1975, *A History of Sufism in Bengal*, Dacca: Asiatic Society of Bangladesh.

Hawley, John S., 2015, *A Storm of Songs: India and the Idea of the Bhakti Movement*, Cambridge, MA: Harvard University Press.

Hawley, John S. and Kenneth E. Bryant, 2015, *Sur's Ocean: Poem's from the Early Tradition* (Murty Classical Library of India), Cambridge MA: Harvard University Press.

Jackson, Peter, 1999, *The Delhi Sultanate: A Political and Military History,* Cambridge: Cambridge University Press.

Jha, Mridula, 2016, 'Mingling of the Oceans: A Journey through the Works of Dara Shikuh', in *Literary and Religious Practices in Medieval and Early Modern India*, ed. Raziuddin Aquil and David L. Curley, New Delhi and London: Manohar and Routledge.

Karamustafa, Ahmet T., 2007, *Sufism: The Formative Period,* The New Edinburgh Islamic Surveys, Edinburgh: Edinburgh University Press.

Kaul, Shonaleeka, 2018, *The Making of Early Kashmir: Landscape and Identity in the Rajatarangini*, New Delhi: Oxford University Press.

Kothiyal, Tanuja, 2016, *Nomadic Narratives: A History of Mobility and Identity in the Great Indian Desert*, New Delhi: Cambridge University Press.

Kugle, Scott, 2016, *When Sun Meets Moon: Gender, Eros and Ecstasy in Urdu Poetry*, New Delhi: Orient Blackswan.

Kumar, Sunil, 2007, *The Emergence of the Delhi Sultanate, 1192-1286,* New Delhi: Permanent Black.

Lal, Ruby, 2018, *Empress: The Astonishing Reign of Nur Jahan*, New Delhi: Penguin.

Lawrence, Bruce B., 1991, *Nizam Ad-Din Awliya: Morals for the Heart,* English translation of *Fawa'd-ul-Fu'ad*, New York: Paulist Press.

Lieberman, Benjamin, 2013, *Remaking Identities: God, Nation, and Race in World History*, Lanham: Rowman & Littlefield.

Lorenzen, David N., 2010, *Nirgun Santon ke Swapana*, New Delhi: Rajkamal Prakashan.

Lutgendorf, Philip, 2016, *The Epic of Ram* (Murty Classical Library of India), Cambridge MA: Harvard University Press.

Madhumalati of Mir Sayyid Manjhan Shattari Rajgiri, English translation by Aditya Behl and Simon Weightman, with Shyam Manohar Pandey, *Madhumalati: An Indian Sufi Romance*, New Delhi: Oxford University Press, 2000.

Malhotra, Anshu, 2017, *Piro and the Gulabdasis: Gender, Sect and Society in Punjab*, New Delhi: Oxford University Press.

Malhotra, Anshu and Farina Mir, 2012, *Punjab Reconsidered: History, Culture and Practice,* New Delhi: Oxford University Press.

Mohan, Sanal P., 2015, *Modernity of Slavery: Struggles Against Caste Inequality in Colonial Kerala*, New Delhi: Oxford University Press.

Mirza, M. Wahid, 1986, *Amir Khusrau*, Delhi: National Amir Khusrau Society.

Mukhia, Harbans, 2004, *The Mughals of India*, London: Blackwell.

Murshid, Ghulam, 2018, *Bengali Culture over a Thousand Years*, translated from the original Bengali, *Hajaar Bochhorer Bangla Samskriti* by Sarbari Sinha, New Delhi: Niyogi Books.

Nahjul Balagha or the Peak of Eloquence, Sermons, Letters and Sayings of Imam Ali ibn abi Talib, English translation by Askari Jafri, part I, Alwaaz International, 2010.

Naim, C.M., 2004, *Urdu Texts and Contexts: The Selected Essays of C.M. Naim*, New Delhi: Permanent Black.

Narang, Gopi Chand, 2017, *Ghalib: Innovative Meanings and the Ingenious Mind*, translated from Urdu by Surinder Deol, New Delhi: Oxford University Press.

Nizami, K.A., 1955, *The Life and Times of Shaikh Fariduddin Ganj-i-Shakar*, Aligarh: Muslim University.

_____, 1991a, *The Life and Times of Shaikh Nasiruddin Chiragh*, Delhi: Idarah-i-Adabiyat-i Delli.

_____, 1991b, *The Life and Times of Shaikh Nizamuddin Auliya*, Delhi: Idarah-i-Adabiyat-i Delli.

Novetzke, Christian Lee, 2008, *Religion and Public Memory: A Cultural History of Saint Namdev in India*, New York: Columbia University Press.

Orsini, Francesca and Samira Sheikh, eds., 2014, *After Timur Left: Culture and Circulation in Fifteenth-Century North India*, New Delhi: Oxford University Press.

Orsini, Francesca ed., 2010, *Before the Divide: Hindi and Urdu Literary Culture*. New Delhi: Orient Blackswan.

Padmavat of Malik Muhammad Jaisi, edited with commentary by Vasudev Sharan Agarwal, Allahabad: Lokbharti Prakashan, 2010.

Pati, Biswamoy, 2019, *Tribals and Dalits in Orissa: Towards a Social History of Exclusion, c.1800-1950*, New Delhi: Oxford University Press.

Petevich, Carla, 2007, *When Men Speak as Women: Vocal Masquerade in Indo-Muslim Poetry*, New Delhi: Oxford University Press.

Rajatarangini of Kalhana, English translation by M.A. Stein, reprint, Delhi: Motilal Banarsidass, 2017.

Richards, J.F., 1991, *The Mughal Empire*, Cambridge: Cambridge University Press.

——, 1997, 'Early Modern India and World History', *Journal of World History*, 8(2): 197-209.

Rao, Velcheru N., David Shulman and Sanjay Subrahmanyam, 2001, *Textures of Time: Writing History in South India*, Delhi: Permanent Black.

Rizvi, S.A.A., 1978, *A History of Sufism in India*, vol. I. *Early Sufism and its History in India to 1600 AD*, Delhi: Munshiram Manoharlal.

Sarkar, Sumit, 2017, *Essays of a Lifetime: Reformers, Nationalists, Subalterns*, Ranikhet: Permanent Black.

Schimmel, Annemarie, 1978, *Mystical Dimensions of Islam*, Chapel Hill: University of North Carolina Press.

Sharma, Manimugdha, 2019, *Allahu Akbar: Understanding the Great Mughal in Today's India*, New Delhi: Bloomsbury.

Sharma, Sunil, 2005, *Amir Khusraw: Poet of Sultans and Sufis*, Oxford: Oneworld Publications.

_____, 2017, *Mughal Arcadia: Persian Literature in an Indian Court*, Cambridge: Harvard University Press.

Sreenivasan, Ramya, 2007, *The Many Lives of a Rajput Queen: Heroic Pasts in India, c.1500-1900*, Seattle: University of Washington Press.

Subrahmanyam, Sanjay, 2010, 'Intertwined Histories: *Cronica* and *Tarikh* in the Sixteenth Century Indian Ocean World', *History and Theory*, 49: 118-145.

Suleiman Charitra of Kalyana Malla, English translation by A.N.D. Haksar, New Delhi: Penguin Books, 2015.

Syros, Vasileios, 2012, 'An Early Modern South Asian Thinker on the Rise and Decline of Empires: Shah Wali Allah of Delhi, the Mughals, and the Byzantines', *Journal of World History*, 23 (4): 793-840.

Tarikh-i-Firuz Shahi of Ziya-ud-Din Barani, English translation by Ishtiaq Ahmad Zilli, Delhi: Primus Books, 2015.

Thapar, Romila, 2013, *The Past Before Us: Historical Traditions of Early North India,* Ranikhet: Permanent Black.

Truschke, Audrey, 2021, *The Language of History: Sanskrit Narratives of Muslim Pasts*, Gurgaon: Penguin Random House.

Vanita, Ruth, 2012, *Gender, Sex and the City: Urdu Rekhti Poetry, 1780-1870*, New Delhi: Orient Blackswan.

Vaudeville, Charlotte, 1993, *A Weaver Named Kabir: Selected Verses with a Detailed Biographical and Historical Introduction*, Delhi: Oxford University Press.

Viitamaki, Mikko, 2016, 'Retelling Medieval History for Twentieth-century Readers: Encounter of a Hindu Prince and a Sufi Master in Khwaja Hasan Nizami's *Nizami Bansuri*', in *Literary and Religious Practices in Medieval and Early Modern India*, edited by Raziuddin Aquil and David L. Curley, New Delhi and London: Manohar and Routledge.

Zaina Rajatarangini of Srivara, English translation by Kashinath Dhar, New Delhi: People's Publishing House, 1994.

Zutshi, Chitralekha, 2017, *Kashmir's Contested Pasts: Narratives, Sacred Geographies and the Historical Imagination*, New Delhi: Oxford University Press.

INDEX